CONTENTS

AKRAM AHMAD

Postcards From The Software Island:
Essays at the Cusp of Ideas, Programming, and Culture

Copyright © 2021 by Akram Ahmad.

FOREWORD

Where We Went Last Time

Y ou may have read my first book—Dispatches from the Software Trenches—the one that's for geeks and non-geeks alike, much as this one is, too: If your interests veer in the direction of the creative, I trust that you fun rummaging through its lavishly illustrated pages. So I was especially flattered to see rave reviews on Amazon, for example:

 Book Nerd

★★★★★ **Thoroughly enjoyable read at the intersection of software and philosophy**
Reviewed in the United States on February 14, 2021
Verified Purchase

A well written and colorful series of essays exploring topics appreciable by the technology-minded and innovation-minded alike.

frances fassett

★★★★★ **A Joyride Through the Trenches!**
Reviewed in the United States on February 13, 2021
Verified Purchase

Akram Ahmad's inimitable style, and his affable, witty approach to technology make these dispatches a pleasure for geeks and non-geeks alike. Don't miss the delightful dispatches and grab a copy of the book today!

Kitty Fassett

 fawad khan

★★★★★ **A wonderful must read!**
Reviewed in the United States on February 10, 2021

Great for practitioner Software engineers and developers!

 Saqib Riaz Qazi

★★★★★ In the age of information overload, Akram's unique writing style is a refreshing change!
Reviewed in the United States on February 16, 2021

Akram always has something to say that gets you thinking, his distinct, genial and conversational approach is endearing and engaging. If anyone has truly experienced the "trenches" starting from the early days of programming the Z80 based ZX Spectrum in Basic and Assembly, its Akram! A book worth reading...

It was a book meant to be enjoyed, *as* is this one!

You *have* read my first book, right? Then again, should this happen to be your introduction to the stuff I write (and to me), allow me to orient you.

How We Got Here

So this whole writing business—using the word "business" in its *enterprising* sense—began with a blog site I created earlier this century, right around 2014. The blog had a singular goal: Create reading material that I couldn't find elsewhere, material that

I wished to read, except that nobody else had written it. So I went ahead and began writing stuff that I wished to read. Honest. (That's the whole story, untenable as it may sound.)

The fact that a ton of people—about 120,000 at my *original* blog and about 40,000-and-counting-and-losing-track-of at my *current* blog site—have taken time out of their precious schedules to read what I write, I can only conclude that the blog has done well. *Really* well.

> *No man is an island, entire of itself; every man is a piece*
> *of the continent, a part of the main.*
> *-John Donne*

How This Book Got Its Name

If the title of my previous book—*Dispatches from the Software Trenches*—conjured up images of drudgery, as if all that we software types did was shovel the trenches, I would be sympathetic with you. (Maybe I should've chosen a *less* somber title for the previous book, my first one.) But I sure hope that your misgivings were laid to rest after you read it: My overall message there, spread out over the eight or so "dispatches from the software trenches"—and I sure hope you took it that way—was intended to be a thoroughly upbeat one. After all, I'm an inveterate optimist.

In hindsight, having seen room for ambiguity, I decided to give *this* book a name that's altogether more radiant than its predecessor's: Instead of the trenches, we get a glorious *island* this time. Woohoo! Life is good. (Yes, the pandemic will end one day; meanwhile, let's keep on with our armchair travels, shall we?)

And yes, even as we dispense with existential issues such as the ones we've skirmished with above—revolve as they do around the theme of ambiguity and fraught as they invariably are with pathways that'll have us burrowing down rabbit holes far too numerous to count—I do want to touch on the *essay* form itself, if only briefly so.

So please don't run away. (We *need* to grapple this trenches-versus-island dichotomy into submission to stay on top. We got this.)

Where We Are Going This Time

A little, island-bird tells me that the book you hold will be the one you take with you if—heaven forbid—you were to get stranded on an island. (I mean, with everyone stuck at home nowadays, doing "staycations," and stuff like that, how likely is that—your getting stranded on an island—to happen anytime soon?)

So yeah, think of this as a grab-bag of goodies, gathered from an excursion; essays, after all, are all about exploring, about chasing ideas, and about pushing our imagination, amirite?

So go ahead and mark this treasue spot (in the island's sublimely-smooth sand, of course) with an *extra*-large X. (We'll need it later.) Meanwhile, we got an oh-so brief exploration coming right up.

Reflections On The Art Of The Essay

And how *did* I get smitten by the essay form? You see, I've been drawn to the essay form for as long as I can remember.

And since the book you hold is all about "postcards"—all hailing from the iconic island of software—ones which we expect to come floating our way soon enough, it behooves us to take a minute or two, and reflect on what makes an essay (aka a "postcard") the unique critter that it is.

To my mind, an essay is first and foremost an attempt to unveil the limits of one's knowledge, with the unstated goal of pushing those limits: To paraphrase ace detective Sherlock Holmes, "*I can't make bricks without hay.*" Montaigne, the father of the modern essay—hailing from yesteryear—would, I think, agree, as would modern day practitioners (of the essay) such as Rebecca Solnit, Dave Barry, Joyce Carol Oates, Paul Graham (*before* his Y-Combinator days, that is), and Anne Fadiman, among others.

"But isn't the essay really an antiquated art form?", you could well ask. A solid question there, and one that I can best answer by pointing to the innumerable blogs that populate the online world, mine among them, I hasten to add: Programming Digressions. The essay is by no means moribund; factor in the vibrant scene on the front of the memoir—a close cousin of the essay—and you begin to see a picture emerge, the picture of an art form that is flourishing by all indications, amirite?

Did Someone Say, "Postcards"?

Closer to home, the theme that binds our postcards—the "essays"—is informed in equal parts by big ideas, by the art of programming, and by culture (plus a smidgen of philosophy sprinkled in here and there.)

"How can such seemingly unrelated themes commingle?", you might ask. Well, recall that man does not live by bread alone; we need butter, too. (Heh, we need each of these three themes—ideas, programming, and culture—in an admixture that leavens our sensibilities even as they give us that spark, and put a zing in our step.)

No Man Is An Island...

I hope you will derive enjoyment from reading this eclectic offering. I had a blast *writing* it up! Oh, and you can read these postcards in any order you wish to; they're totally self-contained, evidently defying John Donne's canon about how

> *No man is an island, entire of itself; every man is a piece of the continent, a part of the main.*

Now the question naturally arises: Which postal service will be *delivering* the postcards?

Maybe it'll be the prim staff of that dainty post office in the quaint British town of Candleford—of the TV series *Lark Rise to Candleford* fame—but I can't say with any certainty. For all I know, our postcards courier may turn out to be the letter-delivering owls from the *Harry Potter* movies.

This I do know: The postcards' source is positively a software island, one inhabited neither by the *Swiss Family Robinson*—or *Robinson Crusoe* for that matter—nor by *Jurassic Park* raptors, but by ideas. This, remember, will be the island to which you'll surely lug along this book, *should* you get stranded during your own travels. (I *hope* you don't, though it'll be good for sales of the book.... Just kidding!)

This Is How We're Going To Do It

Finally, *this* you positively need to know: My writing style is utterly permeated by the sentiment expressed in the following, pithy saying:

> *"My method is to take the utmost trouble to find the right thing to say, and then to say it with the utmost levity."*
> ~ *George Bernard Shaw*

Having described *how* we're going to do it, now we *do* it, starting with an oh-so-brief tick-tock TOC (aka Table Of Contents), like so...

Brief Table of Contents

Here is the proverbial 50,000 feet view of what awaits you in the pages which follow. Here, then, are the marquee names of the eight "postcards"—the eight essays—coming your way:

Postcard I: Supercharge Your Brew Of Ideas

Postcard II: Proactively Reactive

Postcard III: The Programming Imagination

Postcard IV: Best Go Programming Books (2019)

Postcard V: Creativity: All Your Questions Answered

Postcard VI: Tech Gets Lit-Smitten

Postcard VII: To Iterate Is Human

Postcard VIII: Best Scala Books (2019)

With that, I bid you bon voyage. Let's set sail in our navy-blue boats!

◆ ◆ ◆

AKRAM AHMAD

POSTCARD I: SUPERCHARGE YOUR BREW OF IDEAS

0. Intro

Imagination was given to man to compensate him for what he is not; a sense of humor to console him for what he is.
- Francis Bacon

Dear Far-flung Friend,

As I lounge in my lowtide sling beach chair, scribbling down my stream-of-consciousness thoughts within the confined space of the postcard that sits on my lap—the very first of what I intend to be in a series of eight such postcards—my eagerness to meet you knows no bounds. True, we may never meet each other in person, but we will commune all the same; distance may well separate us, my far-flung Friend, but we will bridge that geographic divide with effortless ease.

Not Your Garden Variety Postcard

So yeah, this is not going to be your garden variety postcard... For one thing—based, anyway, on the postcards I've seen in *my* lifetime, leading right up to my getting stranded on this island —these weatherworn and already-tattering postcards simply don't furnish the space to write more than a paltry few sentences. Just saying.
Anyhow, truth being stranger than fiction, an observation transmuted into fact by my being a witness to its veracity, here I am,

sharing some rather personal thoughts on the craft at the cusp of ideas, programming (itself), and culture.

Oh, just so you know, I'm trying really hard to avoid spilling on this postcard any of that delicious coconut juice—the one that I sip straight from a coconut shell—so you, dear Reader, can receive it unbedraggled. (Leave the messy business to me.)

But first, let's segue into some brewing coolness; coconut juice and all can wait for a bit.

What, Exactly, Are We Brewing?

Assuming that you are intrigued by the curious collage in the picture above—notice how the dapper box of tea leaves awaits to be ushered into the bliss of brewing while that towering book next to it boldly proclaims some enigma with a gigantic question mark—the first thing we want to do is situate ourselves regarding what this essay is *not* about.

So, paradoxically enough, we won't delve into the fine art of brewing those alluring tea leaves this time around (that task will await another morning, for example when, heaven forbid, we run out of our trusty *Folgers Choice* coffee crystals.) Nor will we delve into the guts of that question mark-bearing book (*that* will await another leisurely evening when you and I are ready to sit down to a fireside chat.)

Here's What We Will Brew

And with that, it's only fair that you and I hasten to learn what this essay *is* about: This time around, we embark on a slightly —okay, *more* than slightly—discursive exploration of how you can supercharge your very own brew of ideas.

Yeah, anytime you see a picture of either (1) that dapper box of tea leaves, or (2) the upright, question mark-bearing book, you can take that as a memory jog that we're in hot pursuit of brewing ideas.

As for the quote atop this Intro—"*Imagination was given to man to compensate him for what he is not; a sense of humor to console him for what he is*"—I invite you to stay tuned for more on the vital role which (our inner) conversations can play in helping you brew your very own stew ideas.

Finally, if you will humor me—sigh, just one more time—try to imagine what kind of story the following sequence of time-lapse snapshots could be telling.

If you'd rather that I don't leave it your imagination, we have other ways of finding out.

Let's do exactly that.

1. From Inspiration To Idea

People can have many different kinds of pleasure. The real one is that for which they will forsake the others.
- Marcel Proust

Time-Lapse Photography (Take One)

Let's go from left to right in the time-lapse sequence above to see what's up:

Our valiant orange tabby is doing what it does best—being lazy, of course, dreaming away, this time complete with a vacantly indecipherable speech bubble hovering above it—unaware of the brew which awaits its feline senses, its source barely a foot away from its cushy perch.

And then—so this is the **"WHEN SUDDENLY"** part—unbeknownst to tabby, a mysterious benefactor lifts the brew box and tucks it away within the circle of his tawny tail. Tabby wakes up, eyes lit up like embers.

Inspiration descends in a flash—yep, that's the **"ZAP!"** there—and it sure looks like tabby's got his mojo back!

Here it comes—**"POW!"**—valiant tabby is wide awake, ready to rock the world.

Whoah. What just happened?

Time-Lapse Photography (Take Two)

Let's slow it down a notch and take in the time-lapse sequence methodically, gleaning the unstated metaphors at play:

Unbeknownst to onlookers, tabby is actually stewing a brew of deep thoughts in its cranium, percolating away ideas in subliminal fashion. This is the idea-gestation phase.

We all need a helping hand from time to time, and a benefactor is deliciously welcome.

Inspiration strikes unbidden. And this is crucial: When inspiration grabs you, grab it right back.

With your mojo back, it's time to roll.

If that recap of the time-lapse sequence which had preceded it —with us in hot pursuit of divulging the underlying memes and metaphors—was clear as mud, not to worry. What follows is geared for clarifying exactly that.

Put another way, imagine this as a sequence of snapshots:

- This is your life.

- This is your life on *ideas*.

- Any questions?

No questions, eh?

Let's begin.

2. Rev Up Your Idea Factory

Computers are useless. They can only give you answers.
~ Pablo Picasso

Good Fences Make Good Neighbors

I was on the fence when it came to choosing what to call this section: Will it be "The Idea Factory"—which is the name that won out, narrowly—or "Diversify"?

Here's the thing. We all need some kind of generative "source" on our side, a source with which to power our generation of ideas; while creativity is not automatically renewable, it *does* have elements of renewability.

"Okay, Akram, so how do we get a hold of your fabled idea factory?", you ask, and not all that demurely either. Why, glad you did. The short answer is: *"Diversify."* (Hey, I told you it was going to be a *short* answer, amirite?)

Okay, okay, *relax.*

I wouldn't leave you without a fuller answer, would I?

Mere Answers?

So yeah, this is what you should know: Pablo Picasso, the famous artist, sure was on to something vital when, ages ago —in Internet time, that is—he presciently and rather wryly remarked that computers are useless because they give only answers. (Yo, Picasso didn't live to witness the Deep Learning revolution; he might have had a different opinion if he had, and especially if got to see the Deep Fake applied to his beloved world of art. Imagine that. Gulp.)

Anyhow, finding answers to your problems *is* important, especially when the number 42 (as an answer) will not fit the bill—which is, like, pretty much *all* the time.

It turns out that asking the right kind of *questions* if even more important—*far* more important than finding answers.

Enter the idea factory.

Boom! The Idea Factory

And while there's no *postal* address for such an institution, it can be found all around you, eventually distributed in ways both corporeal and ethereal. Put another way, and starting with your public library, extending into the digital realm of the Internet, you'll find resources aplenty with which to set up your very own idea factory—see, my placement of that math book in the cameo pictured above should've alerted you to an imminent book announcement.

Hey, so I chose a *math* book—no questions there, right, as it's literally entitled *The Math Book*—merely to illustrate the notion that ideas are waiting for you in the wings, ready to be plucked and put into the service of realizing your dreams. So go hit up a good book or two that resonate with you, aligned with the themes on your mind of late.

Remember, there's never enough time; there never *will* be enough time.

Go forth and *make* time.

Look up the best of the best (books.) Learn from the masters. (That's what I try to do.)

Diversify

And please do one thing for me: *Diversify.*

Read widely, read *well* outside of your (current) area of specialization. Break down those silos which threaten to isolate us from one another and which would make us the poorer for it; it's time to revise that mindset by becoming less insular.

Let's grow some connective tissue. (More on that in a bit.)

And if you *must* know wherefrom the idea (meme, really) of an idea factory came to lodge itself in the cranium of yours truly —I'm telling you, we've got on our hands a genuinely transportable meme—it is from a namesake book I read nearly a couple of *decades* ago, entitled *The Idea Factory: Learning to Think at MIT* by Pepper White, who entered MIT in 1981 and received his master's degree. (He recounts his experience of attending MIT, and let me tell you: The narrative he weaves is unfiltered, raw, and moving. I have vivid memories of the exact time and place when I read it, ages ago, listening at the same time to the *Yanni* instrumental named *To The One Who Knows*. So now you really, *really* know.)

Some Suggestions

To your list of aids for diversifying, add, for example, listening to soothing—or jazzy, if that be your thing—music, stepping out into the soothing expanse of nature, touching someone's life in an altogether gentle and uplifting way, etc. Don't limit yourself.

The limit, really, and *if* there be one, is your imagination.

Let the world live as one.

Imagine.

AKRAM AHMAD

3. Chase Ideas With A Net

We shall not cease from exploration
And the end of all our exploring
Will be to arrive where we started
And know the place for the first time.
~ T. S. Eliot

Are We In Gotham City, Yet?

Wait, what?

Is that guy on the hillside—you know the one with a ruck-sack on his back and brandishing the heft of a humongous net with the might of both hands—about to haplessly net a.... *bat?!* Gotham City notwithstanding, my spider senses are tingling, compelling me to alert the hapless hunter to the futility of his action.

But I digress.

Speaking of a more relevant (and fruitful) chase, though, have you ever found yourself casting a net of words with which to snare an idea that had popped up in your head, an idea so fleeting that is was ripe for vanishing unless captured in the moment?

But taking a step back, where did the idea come from in the first place? *That's* what we're after. This is heady stuff. Hang tight.

Making Good On A Promise

And before we go there, I need to make good on a promise I had made earlier: In my typical abandon, I had at the outset cited a quote—*"The conversations we have with others end up becoming the conversations we have with ourselves"*—and rather boldly invited you to stay tuned for the scoop on the vital role that conversations can play in helping you brew ideas, amirite?

Yo, there is, but of course, the flip side: Say you are inspired by something you heard or read—take my word and join or start a book club today—and you find yourself inexorably playing with related words, which, unbidden, start to coalesce into the substrate of new ideas. *This* is prime territory for examining and exploring ideas, *not* in isolation, but in tandem, in combination, nay—going one step further—in permutations.

Questions, Deep In Your Eyes

I already see questions swirling deep in your eyes. For example, *"How can my lovely new conceptualization have a prayer of a chance to convey to another the meaning it holds (for me, anyway)?"*

Lovely. You are brilliant, for one thing, and prescient for another.

Modesty forbids, but hey, in full candor—and this is from personal communication—at times when I have, over the years, shared some of my own drafts of writing with Professor Lee (i.e. drafts which subsequently unfurled into some of the essays you've seen posted right here at *Programming Digressions*), he has on occasion oh-so graciously opined that he wished he could write like that. I blush. *He* is a true artist, one of the world's leading educators and researchers in the field of engineering—cyber-physical systems in particular—and a terrific writer on top of all that.

This ethos is about the art of sincere encouragement; at times we find ourselves on the receiving end, and at other times on the giving end. This is also about competition. Most emphatically *not* about competing with one another—now that would be a futile sort of a zero-sum game for which we have no taste—but all about competing with oneself, to see how far we can inspire one another in the pursuit of excellence.

And *that's* what I wished to highlight. Plus, communing

with fiercely-independent, like-minded thinkers makes my day every time.

Define Your Terms, If You Must Converse

A conversation, then—with yourself, with another, or with a book—is that fertile soil in which the seeds of the practice of Art are sown. Contrariwise, the act of expression—in your mind-space, in your writing, and in your speech—is the *harvesting* of the crop that is tilled from the fruits borne by the seeds that were once your own. We gently waft them onto the wings of the harbinger of the wind which has blown.

That is but a glimpse into the commingling of art and expression.

And that, dear reader, is the art of "conversation."

Connective Tissue

Yo, I seldom go this meta—it's not much fashionable anymore, outside of circles of devotees of meta-circular interpreters, amirite? But since I *have*, I might as well conclude by offering some more food for thought:

The phrase "connective tissue"—in the context of organizational topologies—is one that I heard for the first time from another trusted friend. Truth be told, it knocked me out. Flat. A few days ago, I woke up at 2:30 AM, owlishly, and which is when that evocative phrase hit me with the force of a freight train. Splat. Road-kill. *This* is the sort of thing which happens when you're hopelessly—and terminally—in love with words, having surrendered yourself to their irresistible allure.

Hold Your Horses

Look, I've already yammered a bit much, so I'm going to leave another planned foray (into language being the one-and-only vehicle for thought.) Bringing in Friedrich Nietzsche's comments (from his tome entitled *The Will to Power*) on this very subject—that is, how some thinkers have asserted that thoughts are actually nothing but words and language—might be pushing your powers of patience, amirite?

Hey, have you ever heard *me* cry Whorf?

So don't you listen to no siren calls.

Onward.

4. Tend To The Roots (Of Ideation)

It seems as if an age of genius must be succeeded by an age of endeavour; riot and extravagance by cleanliness and hard work.
- Virginia Woolf

What Do We Have Sprouting Here?

Fair warning: Things are about to get pretty leafy. Metaphors are going to sprout, similes will grow untethered—I know, I know that your cheeks are red like a rose and that I'm not as funny as a monkey—and memes will mill around unannounced. (After all, and taking some poetic license, a windmill will not mill around; at least, those critters are not known to, except, that is, in the lexicon of Don Quixote.)

Simile-*shimmy*-lee: As cunning as a fox, you bring up the matter of *Quaker Oats*. (Hmm... Really bad pun. Sorry, Don Quixote.)

Voila! *There* you have the motivation for tending to the roots. Thank you.

Read on to find why (and how) you can do exactly that.

Idle Hands (And Minds) Are...

You can ideate best by keeping your mind active. Here are some strategies—some call them the (mental) daily dozen—to help you achieve mental agility:

- Solve crosswords
- Build jigsaw puzzles
- Flip through some magazines
- Listen to music
- Tackle a Sudoko puzzler

So that's not exactly a dozen, amirite? For crying out loud, that's not even *half* a dozen. (That's only a *starter* list.) So help me fill in the gaps, will you please?

In fact, I have—in invoking the simile that cunning as a fox though I may not be—motivated the admittedly open-ended nature of tending to the roots of ideation: There is no *step*-by-step recipe that'll get you brewing ideas.

Yes, we do have them—those step-by-step recipe—rather nicely regimented in *other* domains. For example, you got programming algorithms, cooking recipes in the culinary arts, directions in navigational systems (a rather fancy reference to Google Maps or its equivalent), etc. But not so when it comes to the realm of brewing *ideas*.

Plus how about the element of elusiveness? (*"Yes, Akram, what about it?"*)

Sheesh.

I was just getting ready to alert you that, at its elemental core —and you're likely sensing that we are navigating our way through uncharted waters—a healthy dose of unpredictability permeates the domain of brewing ideas. - Think espresso coffee.

- Experiment away.

- Build your very own net of activities with which to snare ideas —I know, I know, this is all easier said than done. But you gotta start *somewhere*, amirite?

What Did We Net?

Speaking of nets, would you entertain the idea of netting a butterfly with one. Or would you rather build a perch for that magical bird to alight on? You see, you've come to a fork in the road, ala Robert Frost: You are facing the choice in regards to tackling the quarry—ideas, of course—by either (1) Snaring your quarry, or (2) Inviting it right in, come-into-my-parlor style.

If you catch the drift, what I'm trying to get at is that if you're going to wait for a bird to alight magically, you might as well build a perch for it to alight on.

So get off that couch—more on that soon—and get with the program. Experiment (with idea-generation.) It was free the last time I checked. Plus here's something special I made up just for you. Do try it on for size: A mind in motion can, at times—given the right circumstances—cause quite a commotion.

And be sure to come back and share your very own adventure.

Hey, Did Our Sprouting Experiment Go Haywire?

You see, to tend to the roots, you have to go back to the roots. And don't you dread the spread of the "Triffids" of Sci Fi lore. (Bro, we already got in the COVID-19 pandemic all that we can handle.)

Speaking of the Triffids—those mobile plants with lethal stingers and carnivorous appetites—a copy of John Wyndham's Sci Fi tale (*Day of the Triffids*), which is centered around a freak cosmic event, used to float around in our house back when I was an impressionable lad. You see, my late father, a chemical engineer by profession and an avid Sci Fi fan, occasionally also read material *other* than by his fav, Isaac Asimov. And that reading fare included *Day of the Triffids*, which, at one point, paints a somber scene in darkened London where

> *The gardens of the Parks and Squares were wildernesses creeping out across the bordering streets. Growing things seemed to press out everywhere, rooting in the crevices between the paving stones, springing from cracks in concrete, finding lodgement even in the seats of abandoned cars.*

> *And, of course, over all looms the menace of the rampant triffids, carnivorous plants with an urgent hunger that gives their energy what appears to be a malevolent intelligence.*

And while I stand by my invitation that you tend to your roots, I also urge *some* restraint on your imagination. Of course, if you pay no attention to my advice (regarding restraint) and end up writing another runaway bestseller in the tradition of *Day of the Triffids*, do be sure to remember me.

I will remember you.

Now For The Fauna

Tend to your flora, too; I've heard that *A Tree Grows in Brooklyn*. If the concrete vastness of Brooklyn can afford the irrepressible growth of a tree, then so can you—and me—cultivate such growth by tending to the roots of ideation, amirite?

Wait, coming right next up. That is no flora. It's fauna. And that, too, of the *feline* kind! (*"Felona"*?)

Meow.

5. Stock Up Your Garden (Of Ideas)

A man will turn over half a library to make one book.
~ Samuel Johnson

A Very Selective Club (To Club With)

I would be lying if I told you that there is a royal road to becoming a master of brewing ideas; there just isn't.

You have to go after ideas with a club. (Apologies to Jack London for commandeering one of his memorable quotes, especially since he had put it far more felicitously in remarking that *"You can't wait for inspiration. You have to go after it with a club"*, a quote that I've probably managed to club and bludgeon.)

Having finished tending to the roots of our garden—which is what we did a scant section away—we now turn to *stocking* it up. We want to get to the point where passersby can marvel at our enchanted garden and unabashedly say

> *Mary, Mary, quite contrary*
> *How does your garden grow?*

One more time, if you're going to wait for a bird to alight magically, you might as well build a perch for it to alight on. And here we enter the territory proper of shoring up our stock of ideas. Start by putting your stock in the part having to do with staving off the specter of the utterance that *"Nature abhors a vacuum."*

And here's we are mindful of how, where angels fear to tread, fools rush in. Fools, though, we are not—we're good there, right? —we rush in to fill the vacuum. We don't want to be running dry on ideas. (Imagine that.)

A Subtle Equation

Plus long-time readers know full well that mere cerebral hashing doesn't cut it around here; physicality is part and parcel of the equation. Speaking of equations—and far be it from me to claim that I'm the man who knew infinity—let's channel Robert Frost, who, in his breathtaking essay *The Figure a Poem Makes*, parceled out the equation the best by illumining us that

> *No tears in the writer, no tears in the reader. No surprise for the writer, no surprise for the reader. For me the initial delight is in the surprise of remembering something I didn't know I knew.*

Get physical. Move around and unpack some book-laden boxes; chances are you'll get curious and crack open an intriguing book or two. As you'll witness in the pic above, featuring my feline pal, the idea of unpacking boxes can mean different things to different people (*and* to different species!)

The Nitty Gritty

Reading books—an activity perfectly complemented by the perusal of magazines and blogs such as *Programming Digressions* —will put you ahead of the pack in the area of stocking up your very own garden of ideas.

Hit the books. Don't let any naysayer convince you to sacrifice creativity at the altar of Taylorism—nothing could be more tragic.

So take heart—and paraphrasing from memory the memorable Steve Jobs quote—stay hungry, stay foolish. Search for ideas that *move* you.

An Idea

Many, many years ago—casting about for my bearings as to what America might hold for the newly-arrived immigrant—I was moved by the idea (in a *TIME* magazine article) that in America, what you do *is* what you are.

And that blew my mind.

Yo, ideas that move you are ideas worth pursuing. Do so unabashedly, never forgetting that

> In the beginner's mind there are many possibilities, but in
> the expert's there are few.
> ~ Shunryu Suzuki (author of the most beloved of American Zen books)

Tellingly, the memorable quote above urges you to approach the enterprise of idea stock-up without preconceptions; it is a misconception that (the best) ideas come to insiders, to those who have been "indoctrinated." (Quite the contrary.)

So go out, commune with nature. Commune with books, magazines, blogs. You'll come out stronger.

Don't Forget To Rest, Too

Remember, too, to rest; (new) ideas need downtime for them to take root, to germinate, and to grow. Three words—with apologies to *The Rolling Stones*—may just capture this idea succinctly: *Stock it up!*

Heh, speaking of downtime and rest, checking my feline pal, valiant hunter that he is—at least he works on keeping that *air* about him—partaking of well-earned rest, lounging in his perch, tucked away in the background to the facade that is the duo of (1) a fine specimen of framed, cross-stitch wizardry, and

(2) a tea leaves-bearing *Ahmad Tea* box.

What brews ahoy?

6. Get Off That Couch (Or, Turn Off The TV)

I must say I find television very educational. The minute somebody turns it on, I go into the library and read a good book.
~ Groucho Marx

Do I, Or Don't I?

I was torn. Do I spill the beans and tell you exactly how I feel about the (anti) role / place that the couch—along with its equally insidious partner the TV—have in my lexicon, making myself unpopular like dickens? Or do I tiptoe around this one, sugar-coating the truth?

Divulging the unvarnished truth—at least as yours truly sees it —is what won out in the end. I stand by what I've said in the past: A writer sticks his or her neck out. She is never for sale because, through her writings, a writer sticks her neck out, knowing full well that her neck may well get wrung. But she is brave; she *has* to be bold.

That, then, is the essential experience and which, put another way, informs you that

> *You don't have to burn books to destroy a culture. Just get people to stop reading them.*
> *- Ray Bradbury*

But I digress, though I suspect that the specter of possibly getting drawn and quartered is not *all* that appealing to you; it sure isn't to me. But yeah, divulging the unvarnished truth—that getting off the couch is crucial—is what we just finished doing.

And here, your faith will see you through.

The Unreasonable Effectiveness Of Leaving That Couch

So why, *exactly*, is getting off that couch crucial?

Here's why: As I've held forth on this very subject, you and I are not getting very far without enlisting the aid of this critter that goes by a rather cryptic name: working memory.

"Akram, are you going to upset the apple-cart yet again?"

Darn.

I knew *somebody* was going to say that!

A Critter We've Met In The Past

Look, the deal here—and I urge you again to check the scoop on this working memory critter—is that our minds, awash as they are in the ceaseless abundance of information, need time (and scaffolding) for ideas to take root and germinate. (Otherwise, we get down to a RAM-style operational style, aka *modus operandi*: Disconnect our access to the deluge of information—yes, that would be the Internet—and we beguilingly blink our eyes in hapless defenselessness. YMMV.)

That's right.

Let's say we're cooking up (aka brewing) an algorithm in our head, adding in the details, bit by bit—or "thimbleful by thimbleful," as Nicholas Carr memorably puts it in his superb book *The Shallows: What the Internet Is Doing to Our Brains*. Take away this crucial activity of scaffold-creation (tending to ideas by attending to them—really attending to them as if your life depended on it—by making time in the first place for the activity of fitting new ideas into your universe of knowledge), and you basically shoot yourself in the foot.

This Is What You'll Do

So turn off the Internet for a bit—I know full well just how un-comfortable it feels—and make time for ideas to take root and germinate.

So get off that comfy Posturepedic couch, turn off the TV, and start rolling. (A mind in motion belongs to a person—you, of course!—who is going places. And here I fell a tinge of remorse: I keep adding to your ever-growing list, but that's what you get for having me as a friend, amirite?)

Get *active*.

Imagine buzzing around like a honeybee, sipping drops of nec-tar from this source and that, from here and from there, prac-ticing the alchemy of turning ideas into the honey of insight and original knowledge. (Never you mind the pollen issues; we're conveniently sweeping those under the rug, where they'll stay, snug as a bug.)

Or perhaps imagine being a spark-plug—I know, I know, this is right up there with the equally meta pronouncement that *"There is no spoon"*—making connections, and possibly even ig-niting a revolution in the realm of human thought.

The Heart Of The Matter

Remember, though, my (famous) last words, if it came down to that: I truly love you and write to serve you. I write for you just as much as I write for myself. (Shh... I write stuff that I wish people would write; since *they* don't—at least not half as often I wish they would—*I* do.) You have rewarded me by coming back time and time again, sometimes sharing your thoughts via soul-ful comments, melting my heart in the process.

But get off that couch you *must*. (Thank you, master Jedi Yoda, for perpetuating your meme of inimitably phrasing things, ri-tornello-style.)

(Hmm... My feline pal now comes into view—wow, he sure has shiny embers for eyes!—all curled up, and that, too, upside-down fashion, slouching away, *couching* away. Evidently, *he* didn't get the memo.)

7. Look With New Eyes

*The real voyage of discovery consists, not in seeking new
landscapes, but in having new eyes.*
~ Marcel Proust

Grab That Life-Jacket

How can one possibly keep up with the deluge of information
swirling around us all, threatening at times to drown us with
its power of inundation? We all become speed readers? But that
would be to court a fate similar to Woody Allen's when he wryly
observed how

> *I took a speed-reading course and read "War and Peace" in
> twenty minutes. It involves Russia.*

What *does* one do, then?
Enter the kingdom of ideas, and in particular this one from
that realm by one of the world's most prolific—and beloved—
writers, Isaac Asimov, when he shared the following observation, one that I'm allowing to speak for itself:

> *I am not a speed reader. I am a speed understander.*

Loved it! Plus a healthy dollop of creativity is always helpful,
because

> *We cannot solve our problems with the same level of
> thinking that created them.*
> *~ Albert Einstein*

Yes, look with new eyes. Plus, if you wish to turn *your* world upside-down—and turn *the* world upside-down in the process —keep in mind the principles of creative thinking, with the theme of divide-and-conquer in tow.

A Curious Mix

Caution: We're about to enter the realm of tangerine trees and marmalade skies...

To use the metaphor of the kaleidoscope, what with all its marvelously-loopy powers of refraction, would be to court digression: Ouch. I bit my lip as I said that. (Oh, the things I do—*and* don't do—just for you.)

> *Explaining Metaphysics to the nation–*
> *I wish he would explain his Explanation*
> *~ Lord Byron (from Don Juan: Dedication)*

One more thing. It will be to your advantage to remember that specialization leads to fragmentation. ("*Now what does that have to do with look with new eyes?*" you inquire, vehemently.) Allow me to explain.

Our best bet when it comes to grappling with the looming crisis of complexity is to specialize. ("*Akram, for crying out loud, didn't you just finish telling us that specialization leads to fragmentation? And now you tell us to, um, specialize!*")

Gah! What to do?

Here's what: In a nutshell, we're working with an essentially intrinsic human limitation, that of how much we can stash away in the chalkboard of our cranium. (Oh yeah, it's that working memory critter coming back to bite us again. Ouch.)

But fear not: To be forewarned is to be forearmed, amirite?

This Is Your Moment To Shine

Armed with this knowledge, go forth and create greatness in your field. Don't get rule-bound. (Hey, algorithms are great, so don't get me wrong; plus they keep getting more and more intelligent every day.) So take inspiration from what it means when

> *Works of art make rules; rules do not make works of art.*
> ~ *Claude Debussy*

Goodness, what's up with the scene we now see appearing on the horizon? (Our valiant cat is back. This time, though, he ain't got no shiny embers for his eyes... For crying out loud, he is *surrounded* by shiny embers, all aglow in luminous unison.)

Is that you in the picture, Professor McGonagall? (Also, and *just* checking, in case you had plans of vanishing on the spot. You're sure not grinning in the pic, so you couldn't be the Cheshire Cat: either. Elementary, my dear Watson.)

Onward.

8. Farewell (For Now)

The golden age is before us, not behind us.
- William Shakespeare

Why Should Parting Be Such Sweet Sorrow?

We have now come to the end of the journey. (It could've been worse: We could've come to the end of *our* tether.)

I will leave you with but one thought. (*"Akram, you sure? You really, really sure?"*) Ah, my reputation to digress precedes me, yet again.

Heh.

Here is that thought: Proceed from first principles in all your endeavors, including the one of brewing ideas. Remember that

> *Logic will get you from A to B. Imagination will take you everywhere.*
> *- Albert Einstein*

Now Einstein was one cool—and very smart—cookie.

First Principles (Called That For A Reason)

In the same vein—that of proceeding from first principles in all your endeavors—remember, too, that

> *Education is an admirable thing, but it is well to remember from time to time that nothing that is worth knowing can be taught.*
> *~ Oscar Wilde*

Finally—yo, I'm *really* sure this time—I would be remiss if I didn't paraphrase Natalie Goldberg, one of my favorite writers, when she observed that first thoughts have enormous energy, and your job is to harness those first flashes when your mind is on to something. There is, in all of us, this inner censor which squashes those first thoughts: What we end up with is living in the echoes of second and third thoughts, rarefied.

So yeah, ask a more beautiful question.

Diversify and light up your world.

Brew some ideas.

◆ ◆ ◆

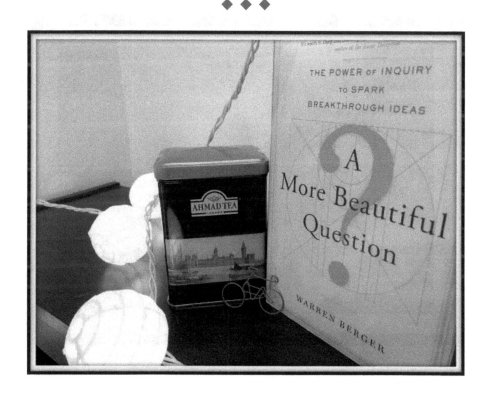

POSTCARD II:
PROACTIVELY
REACTIVE

1. Intro

The future is already here—it's just not very evenly distributed.
~ William Gibson

D

ear Far-flung Friend,

It is my fond hope that you got my prior postcard—the inaugural one—safe and sound. What I have found, meanwhile, is this cathartic expanse open up as I shared my thoughts with you. And much as I had noted in that postcard, my eagerness to meet you knew no bounds; it still doesn't.

Eager To Meet You

If anything, I'm even *more* eager to learn what you thought of the beginnings of our communing; I'll wait for your reply. (I'm still trying to figure out the zip code of this forsaken island, one that time evidently forgot, as did our trusty postal service. Sigh, you can count on them.)

Anyhow, while walking on the beach of this software island, one that's situated squarely in an arrestingly magnificent archipelago, I got excited as my mind turned to all things reactive.

I Scribble Away

So here I am, scribbling down some more musings, the better to share with you; what good are they, after all, if you remain unaware. With that, it is my fond hope—especially given the paradigmatic nature of the subject matter this time—that you will derive some value.

(And yes, I'll be sure to follow up with our postal service so you can become privy to this island's zip code. Hmm... Since this happens to be an *archipelago*, I wonder if USPS can split the zip code. Sigh. Complications.)

But let's keep our poise. Who know, one day we'll even become card-carrying members of the vaunted postal society, joining the fine ranks of the prim staff which deck that dainty post office in the quaint British town of Candleford, of the TV series *Lark Rise to Candleford* fame.

Card-Carrying Member, Eh?

Meanwhile, as a card-carrying member of the reactive programming community—so I became a signatory several years ago on the Reactive Manifesto—I have put into practice its tenets plus seen firsthand the evolving landscape of our software industry reap the benefits of embracing the reactive programming paradigm.

And as someone who eats, drinks, and breathes the reactive programming paradigm, I've recently followed with great excitement something big—and I mean really big in terms of a brand new investment—unfold before my eyes over the past week.

Ever so often, we get to witness thoughtful industry leaders nudge our industry in exactly the direction in which it needs to go. These are leaders who, in addition to being in the vanguard of industry captains, also happen to be incredibly tech-savvy, having been there in the tech trenches themself and having made substantial contributions to the corpus of software deployed out there, software that undergirds the digital fabric of modern life.

Ah, and allow me to elaborate; I purposely chose William Gibson's prophetic words atop (*"The future is already here—it's just not very evenly distributed"*) to illustrate what I have in mind. Read on to find out.

2. Released From The
Shackles Of Constraints

I n shepherding the brand new investment I referred to earlier, leadership has played a pivotal role in helping usher in the future of a "more-evenly distributed" reactive future. It sure has got this technologist excited. *Really* excited.

What, *Me* Digress?

Notwithstanding my propensity for, um, digressing at length when it comes to the vital topics that bedeck our professional world of software—and you are likely all too familiar with the passion that fuels me in this realm—I feel compelled to convey the impact of this move. So here's the deal. With cloud native application development having become quite the ascendant rocket, which it deserves to be, this move is poised to show the world how things should—and *will*—be done, going forward.

Just to remind you, the sensible handling of currency in software development is paramount. It weighs heavily on our minds—much more so today than it ever has before—as we navigate our way through a multicore world. Nobody argues with that.

Then we throw some eventual consistency in there. And oh my, the fun we get to have. Nobody argues with that either!

And so it is that the reactive programming paradigm—it once used to be on the fringes of the programming community—became mainstream, having been widely and warmly embraced the world over.

Seriously, Though

It would be more accurate—and referring here to the heading atop this section—to say that several crucial software development constraints have been wrangled into submission. But that is oh-so Kafkaesque. So yeah, we no longer have to treat concurrency as the intractable, wild beast we had begrudgingly gotten to know concurrency as, and instead treat it on *our* terms.

How so? Glad you asked. We'll meet you on the other side of the fabulous cantilever of a bridge coming right next up.

3. Building A Bridge To The Future

Glad you made it here. But, yes, the question looms as large as ever: How do we get there, as we travel along the reactive road? Well, for starters, a substantial body of knowledge has been assembled over the years, a good portion of which I've been covering here on this blog. For example, check these musings:

- The Reactive Programming Mindset

- Some More On The Reactive Programming Mindset

- A Bit About The Underlying Philosophy

So *that's* how we do it.

Should you wish to arm yourself with even more knowhow, I suggest you check this out and get a fuller story.

Oh, and speaking of what I had earlier called a "more-evenly distributed" reactive future, I'm willing to wager that William Gibson's prophetic words—*"The future is already here; it's just not very evenly distributed"*—are finally going to see the light of day.

Let's make this happen!

4. Unpacking The Phrase
"Proactively Reactive"

But first, we got some unpacking to do. And this has nothing whatsoever to do with our intrepid sleuth Tintin. You'll spot him make a cameo appearance—standing atop a stack of tape-flags-aglitter books on a desk in my study—standing shoulder-to-shoulder with an admittedly oversized teapot, whose caffeinated content just might come in handy, should you wish to zip through those books in a sitting (or two).

Unpacking The Meaning

Seriously, though, the *unpacking* I've got in mind has to do with those two words—"Proactively Reactive"—yep, the ones I chose for the very name of this essay.

So yes, instead of having me take you on a deep-dive through the offerings in the marvelous books stacked up above—and there's *many* an oyster and other assorted treasures to be found in there—let's settle for the distillation thereof, which I've done just for you, that distillation coming up over the span of the next four sections.

Cool?

And while that pile of ragtag, tape-flags-aglow books may appear somewhat random, the *hardcover* standing upright (containing the erudite, collected works of America's laureate of light verse, Ogden Nash) is definitely not random; it's got a mission in life, and will serve a vital purpose in just a few. Stay tuned, won't you?

So yeah, mentally prepare yourself to witness some unpacking take place before your eyes—remember, we'll be unpacking that fecund phrase "Proactively Reactive" over the course of this essay—my aim being to model that unfolding on the graceful blooming of a rose under time-lapse photography.

Ah, one more thing: My use of the word *unpacking* may perhaps have led your fine logical mind to launch a reflexive exploration of the programming construct we know (and love) as *destructuring*. It serves a useful purpose...

But I digress.

5. A Community Of Growth

When it comes to capturing the gist of evolving software architecture and design, all kinds of metaphors—cities, buildings, communities—have been bandied around over the years. All (generally) good, all (mostly) sensible. But to get to the heart of the matter, looking for the beauty in this all, let's pause and think about the people behind the growth. Yes, exactly, communities of people are what principally matter. The engines of growth are squarely centered in that area.

So it is especially heartwarming to witness precisely this kind of leadership on display in the context of forging alliances which, IMHO, are destined to propel our industry forward in the relentless quest to keep moving in the right direction.

Put the right technology in the hands of the right people, in your cooking with gas. But what do I know?

Actually, I *do* know a thing or two (maybe even *three!*) And that —the heart of the programming paradigm I have in mind—is what we get to check out next.

6. Reactive Software Is Responsive

The crux of the matter when it comes to this aspect of reactive architectures is that software systems had better respond in a timely manner. Terrific responsiveness—zippiness if you will—translates into terrific usability. Even more so, when a software system is responsive, it means that problems get detected rapidly whereby problems can be nipped in the bud.

Well, guess what? All this translates into simplified error-handling, which, in turn, boosts the confidence of users. Think happy customers.

7. Reactive Software Is Message-Driven

I was initially going to name the section-heading above "Reactive Software Is Asynchronous And Message-Driven". But it came across as unwieldy, a bit of a sprawl, shall we say. Come to think of it, let me ask you: Spatially speaking at least, ever heard of the venerable Mall of America, the largest mall in the US, being called not a mall but the sprawl?

But I digress.

While we're chatting up my home state (Minnesota), and should you wish to find out what happened *"One Winter's Morning (in Minnesota)"*, you can do so now. That's quite all right, we'll wait for you while you take that brief detour.

Ah, you're back. Good. Let's move right along.

8. Reactive Software Is Elastic

First things first: I don't know about you, but I sure don't want to find myself ever within a one-mile radius of the whale shark ahoy. Check the pic above. Methinks—at least judging by the supremely chapped lips of that lumbering oceanic giant—it could use some lip balm. I mean, ChapStick, Vaseline, something! Frankly, you would think that with all the megatons of water in the ocean deep, that whale could keep its lips moist. But oh no, ChapStick it is that its little heart desires.

Whale, At Starboard

And the mouth to which those lips are attached is demonstrably elastic. Ever witnessed a whale shark open its mouth— without any signs of stopping—to take in the plankton that is its primary diet? Yeah, that's what the experts say anyway. But I ain't taking no chances; I'm plenty happy to watch that ocean giant swimming from after, like *really* afar.

Anyhow, what I really wanted to say about this particular aspect of reactive software is that the goal here is to keep systems responsive under varying workload. This translates into dollars and cents: Reactive Systems can respond to fluctuations in user requests by increasing or decreasing the resources deployed to service those request. Yep, we get to have cost-effectiveness, on _commodity_ hardware platforms.

9. Reactive Software Is Resilient

Ever seen a seemingly-dead, leaden landscape in winter come to life with the burgeoning of the spring season? So that's what I had in mind in selecting the picture above. Hey, is anyone even noticing my thematic artwork—the painstakingly-selected public-domain pictures that I've endearingly framed in delicate borders after running each one through a filter—or will I again find myself tracing (yet again) the tracks of my tears?

Lest We Forget

While your tender heart attends to that matter, allow me to slip in a few words edgewise. For example, we in the reactive programming community aim for software systems to stay responsive in the face of the inevitable failures; they come with the territory of cloud native applications. Replication, containment, isolation, and delegation help us build resilience into systems.

Hmm... I wonder if that's an aerial view of Wisconsin, the dairyland of America? Either way, if ever you wondered about the design philosophy that underlies and, in fact, powers every conceptual aspect of reactive programming, you positively need to read the next section—I heard someone say, *"Don't you let Akram start waxing philosophical about anything software-related, because we've seen for ourselves, many times over, how he can turn into an Energizer bunny every time he does that!"*

I didn't hear that.

10. Actors, or All The
World's But A Stage

Pure and simple, this is the marvelous realm of akka.io. Some have said that this is object-orientation done right. And I agree. Oh yes, it's message-passing all the way down.

Since I've written at length on this topic *elsewhere*, it strikes me as most efficient to point you in the direction of one such musing.

11. Setting Sail For The Fabled Island

Are we there yet? Have we alighted on the fabled utopia of software bliss?

Somebody? Anybody?

Well, it turns out that there's no silver bullet, but we sure get closer and closer to finding it, to making it happen.

Oh yes. Wicked though the problems may be, we software practitioners are getting better and better at being prepared to take them on with increased confidence, thanks in (large) part to the principles and practice of the reactive paradigm.

It just so happens that the decidedly effective design methodology of *Domain-Driven Design* (aka *DDD*) fits hand-in-glove with the reactive paradigm; I've seen and done it for myself. In fact, a bunch has been written on *DDD*, with myself, too, having made some contributions to the practice and dissemination of DDD.

12. Reactive Happenings

When it comes to rubber meeting the road, the reactive style of architecture has got rock-solid support in the Scala programming language. Don't get me wrong: You can use just about any programming language—okay, maybe not assembly language—to support the reactive style. It's just that my experience with Scala (over the past eight years or so) has got me convinced me that Scala is a match made in heaven when it comes to making the widespread adoption of reactive architectures a reality.

The Community

The Reactive Summits are awesome events where the reactive community comes together in person. Most recently, I attended Reactive Summit 2017 (in Austin, Texas). It was a blast. Next up, I was getting ready to attend Reactive Summit 2018 (in Quebec, Canada) but ended up going to another awesome event (Open IoT Europe 2018), where I also had a blast, which I chronicled here.

Returning to the present moment, I'm genuinely excited by what I earlier referred to as leadership on display, leadership and alliances that are poised to help usher in the future of a "more-evenly distributed" reactive future.

It is my fond hope that I've managed to convey the essence of how the *call* of cloud native application development—a style that's becoming increasingly pervasive in our industry—will be *answered* by reactive architectures, ably guiding us in a multi-core world.

You, Too?

Is there something *you* can do?

Oh yeah, and glad you asked. Check the billboard coming right up on the horizon as we barrel down the road. And we'll meet you on the other side (of the billboard, of course).

13. Go Ahead And Sign That Billboard

Aha, so that was just to grab your attention—and what better to do that than by making mention of those ubiquitous billboards that line your typical roadside. And no worries, I'm going to make this easy for you: No need to brace yourself for the formidable climb up the billboard scaffolding, with or without the help of that rather rickety and precariously perched 20 foot ladder!

All you have to do is head over there and have a look at the Reactive Manifesto, and then embellish it with your lovely signature. That's all. See, didn't I tell you I was going to make this easy?

14. And Witness The Transformation

So this one you'll just have to experience for yourself to see what I've been getting at over the span of this essay: Embracing the reactive paradigm will garner spectacular results when it comes to achieving your software development goals.

It's been said that "*The best way to predict the future is to invent it*". With the best practices, scaffolding, and infrastructure—for all things reactive—in place, you have but to take the next step and try it out for yourself. Much as I said above, this one you'll just have to experience for yourself to get the full import.

It will be well worth your while!

Star Wars And Such

Wait a sec, and speaking of the future, what in the world is that futuristic behemoth of a whale—goodness, it *is* a whale, and of the *Star Wars* kind, too—doing here, coming into our view right next up? This isn't quite what I had in mind when I quoted a minute ago about how "*The best way to predict the future is to invent it*".

Methinks I need to revisit my formula for blending OO and FP, or something.

But I digress.

AKRAM AHMAD

15. Swimming With The Best

Animals are such agreeable friends—they ask no questions, they pass no criticisms.
- George Eliot

As we call it a wrap, and this is especially for those of you who had earlier taken in the sight of the ragtag stack of books on the brown desk in my study and perked up—even more so, in fact, by the sight of the hardcover standing guard over the stack, holding between its two sturdy covers the collected works of America's laureate of light verse, Ogden Nash—your moment has finally arrived.

Erudition

So let's see, with your having taken a peek at Nash's erudition, by way of the splendid poem quoted above, what do you think? Are you *still* game for taking a dip in the ocean with one of those lumbering giants swimming a few feet away?

Speaking for myself—and should I somehow end up in the maw of that oh-so gentle giant above or, for that matter, the one cruising in the picture below, though it really doesn't matter *which* one of the two—it's going to get a tad complicated to do my reactive designs and programming from in there. I think I'm good with (and especially on) *terra firma*.

I wish you every success on your reactive journey. Do please write back. We all would love to hear from you!

POSTCARD III: THE PROGRAMMING IMAGINATION

0. Hello World (Redux)!

To see the world in a grain of sand, and to see heaven in a wild flower, hold infinity in the palm of your hands, and eternity in an hour.
- William Blake

Dear Far-flung Friend,

Yay! It's time for our third postcard. And we're going to have some fun this time: Get ready to let your imagination roam. We're about to look (anew) at the world of computing like it's never been witnesed before.
I've got stuff here with which I fervently wish to give wings to *your* imagination. So there; I said that.

Warming Up

But first, should you be ready for some mental calisthenics—yo, a quick trip to the online dictionary confirms that I'm correctly recalling this million-dollar word as standing for "gymnastic exercises to achieve bodily fitness and grace of movement"— let's get some warm-up going:

1. When someone (not you, of course!) throws all concerns for a properly designed domain model—*and* caution—to the wind, what they are likely to end up with is a case of *nickel*-cell anemia. Now we're limbering up, though I'd rather we also jettison off all things anemic!

2. Moving along to a more light-hearted calisthenic, let's ponder on what one might call a Neanderthal who is prone to meandering... Hmm... Hey, a *Meanderthal*, but of course! (For the low down on this, look no further than Item #14—OF MEANDERING NEANDERTHALS—in another essay entitled *Domain-Driven Design (DDD) Defies Dogma*)

3. Now, should Miss Ann—she of the Green Gables—throw a small, green, and globular vegetable in a fit of hysteria, and I happen to be observing her act of flinging the hapless vegetable (slap on the wrist for doing that, Miss Ann, slap on the wrist), would you stop me from dubbing Miss Ann's *Breakfast Club*-inspired act as one of misanthropy?

Okay, *okay*, I get the less-than-subtle signals to quit this calisthenics thing—Hey, are you all, like, a bunch of couch potatoes or something?! Not you, dear Reader, *them*... But... Just *one* last calisthenic (I promise!) and I'm out of here...

4. So, what quandary might we need to get ourselves out of, should we find our sorry rears in the fine land of Decatur (in the realm of Africa to be sure) where we need to indicate that our car is ready to make a turn at the road intersection we're fast approaching? May I suggest an *indicator*—we're in Decatur, for crying out loud—even as I stave off howls of lachrymose, existential angst from readers *just* like you.

Now We're Ready

Woohoo! Warmed up by those mental gymnastics—at one level, those were merely neologisms I whipped up, but, whatever—we're ready. Let's go.

Welcome Back, You All

Oh, and totally by the way, hey, welcome right back to our *new* blog site, with the second brand new essay written just for our new digs (I sure was pleased when I noticed that the blog visitors counter had soared past the 100,000 mark just the other day: Thank you all, you keep me going!)

AKRAM AHMAD

1. The Network Is The Computer

Questions are never indiscreet, answers sometimes are.
- Oscar Wilde

A classic case of how chance ever favors the prepared mind—especially as we just treated ourselves to a blast from the past in the lacunae and life of the discoverer of the principles of vaccination and microbial fermentation—surely has to be this thing about how "the network is the computer." I mean...

Okay, so this goes back to the days when mention of the word "intranet" led to heretical pronouncements of typos; people blithely reading magazine ads thought the jingo was meant to say "internet"! But the visionaries stuck to their tasks, feverishly weaving the loom of the modern digital world—never taking their eyes off the wisdom of Alan Kay's words that "The best way to predict the future is to invent it"—and did not rest until they had put the fully woven fabric of that world in our outstretched hands.

2. On The Unbearable
Lightness Of Atomicity

Insanity is often the logic of an accurate mind overtasked.
- Oliver Wendell Holmes

Yo, we tread here on delicate ground. So, shall we make sure to get this right, lest our ship ran aground? Object are created, before being found; immutable variables bound; remember, though, that divide-by-zero errors simply can't be rounded down; so check out how pure functions are born, healthy and sound. Yeah, this ain't no pitcher's mound; a tad tinged, I do confess, by sleuth-work we've come to associate with that inimitable crime-hunter who appeared, for example, in the tale of the Baskerville hound.

Hey now, the rhyme here is getting out of bound... (And I sure ain't ready for another core dump of memory, or a hairy stack trace or, sheesh, an exception message profound!)

Dear Reader, turn around...

Check this—trust me, this is not a random suggestion!—and I'll give you my penny for your pound: *When Object Orientation Met Functional Programming*

(Oh, did I forget to tell you about *another* great deal—in addition to the one above about how I'll give you my penny for your pound—having to do with the Brooklyn Bridge going on sale, and that a better deal than it simply can't be found?)

3. Engage Your Senses (All Of Them)

Your theory is crazy, but it's not crazy enough to be true.
~ Niels Bohr

Not to worry: Relax, we are not planning on invoking college—
or even high school—Physics, should that subject have brought
about a Maalox moment or two in your life. For advice and resources on cultivating this aspect of the imagination, look no
further than the section on the work of David Perkins (over
yonder in MA, on the other side of Charles River, specifically in
the Harvard Graduate School of Education), and which had appeared—I mean, I know it, because I wrote it!—many moons ago
at these coordinates: Top Thought Leaders to Follow

4. Some Things Are Negotiable
(Others, Not So Much)

Content negotiation is useful. One use is to shepherd a new data format into a world which initially does not typically accept it. It allows those systems which do accept the new format to advertise it and so participate in the new technology.
~ Sir Tim Berners-Lee (on the finer points of Content Negotiation)

Should you find yourself haggling for a good deal in the market-lined streets, may I suggest that you remember Sir Tim Berners-Lee's aforementioned wise words: Yes, transplanted—hook, line, and sinker—straight from the world of bits and bytes to the real life. Here is what you need to do... Check this. Read it. I'll wait for you...

Hello? Still reading? Ah, that quite all right. Keep smiling, and carry right on.

5. Try Your Hand At (Some) Lyricism

My own brain is to me the most unaccountable of machinery—always buzzing, humming, soaring roaring diving, and then buried in mud. And why? What's this passion for?
- Virginia Woolf

Lyricism is the heart and soul of the imagination. Period. Take this from me—someone who has been there and done that—to mean that if *I* can do it, so can you!

Okay, should you be feeling bold enough to find out everything you ever wanted to know about lyricism (but were afraid to ask), check out these unfiltered, straight-from-the-gut series of discourse:

- On Writing: Or *Why* I Write

- On Writing: Or *How* I Write

- On Writing: Or *Wow* I Write

- On Writing: Or *Now* I Write

- On Writing: Or A *Row* With *How* I Write

The imagination of yours truly is unabashedly on display at the coordinates above, all five of them; proceed, dare I add, at your own risk...

Enough for now? Cool, I *thought* that would do. For now, anyway, right?

6. Follow The Signposts...

If the path be beautiful, let us not ask where it leads.
- Anatole France

Harking back to the words ("The future is already here—it's just not very evenly distributed") of the "noir prophet" of the cyberpunk sub-genre of science fiction (William Gibson), what conclusion(s) can you draw right this second?

I'm waiting, no rush. Please take your time... Tick, tock. Tick, tock...

◆ ◆ ◆

POSTCARD IV: BEST GO PROGRAMMING BOOKS (2019)

0. Intro

If you tell the truth, you don't have to remember anything.
- Mark Twain

D ear Far-flung Friend,

How time flies... My mental muscles had started getting flabby when I shook myself from a reverie—I'm telling you, this island has its allure, but it comes with the price of remaining vigilant to its hypnotic and mind-numbing powers. Yep, on regaining a modicum of alertness, it dawned on me that it was already time to send a *fourth* postcard your way.

Approaching Cruising Altitude

We're at the halfway mark as we wend our communing journey through the series of eight postcards. So without further ado, let's get sharp and check a marvelous language that you don't want to miss, whether you're stranded on an island—*I* sure am— or not.

Yep, that sure is my place and position. Speaking of which, one's station and positin in life, and without a shadow of doubt, Go is extremely well-positioned to be the go-to language for writing modern (and maintainable!) programs which can tackle head-on the unique challenges introduced by mushrooming in-frastructure that operate at massive scales. Yep, I can tell from first-hand experience (over the past one year) that Go's got what it takes to meet the demands for delivering on highly scalable, ruthlessly efficient (and sanely maintainable!) software to keep up with user demands.

A Little Bird Told Me

In case you haven't noticed—and hey, no worries if you haven't! —two colorful *introductions* to (well, more like *adventures* in) have already appeared earlier on our digs here:

- *The Go Programming Language*

- *Further Adventures In Go Land*

Rest assured: No boring treatise (on Go language arcana or stuff like that) will be found in either of the aforementioned intros. Just a couple of no-holds-barred cruises through the rollicky landscape of Go.

1. What's Coming Up?

So let's see how the talk so far (aka the preamble) shapes up in this post because—more so than in any earlier blog post—I'm taking inspiration this time from the inimitable Irish playwright and polemicist George Bernard Shaw when he spilled his beans and said that, "My method is to take the utmost trouble to find the right thing to say, and then to say it with the utmost levity."

And yeah, don't you just take my word for it; read on to find out how *you* can benefit today from what I have to offer: In casting a glance back at my (ongoing) journey to Go enlightenment, here's my take on how (and exactly *why*) a handful of books have proven incredibly helpful to me.

2. The List

So I'm about to take an opinionated look at each one of the following books, in turn:

- *The Go Programming Language* by Alan A. A. Donovan and Brian W. Kernighan (Addison-Wesley Professional Computing Series)
- *Learning Functional Programming in Go* by Lex Sheehan (Packt Publishing)
- *Go in Action* by William Kennedy, Brian Ketelsen, Erik St. Martin (Manning Publications)
- *Programming in Go: Creating Applications for the 21st Century* by Mark Summerfield (Addison-Wesley Professional)
- *Concurrency in Go: Tools and Techniques for Developers* by Katherine Cox-Buday (O'Reilly Media)
- *Go in Practice: Includes 70 Techniques* by Matt Butcher, and Matt Farina (Manning Publications)
- *Go Web Programming* by Sau Sheong Chang (Manning Publications)

My hope is that you'll thereby be armed with the knowledge of which Go resources to get your hands on (to help you grok Go at *your* own pace.)

3. Atmospheric (Barometer) Check

Know, too, that I've taken great care in preparing the atmosphere (yeah!) in each one of the (soon-to-appear) pictures in this post.

The goal: Make your cruise through the rollicky landscape of Go enjoyable! And if you really must know more about those two figurines—the iconic British telephone booth and Tintin the sleuth—in the topmost picture (plus in a bunch of upcoming ones), such as where came from, then I refer you to Yer Edinburgh Ode to Microservices for the unabridged, gory details, which are way too much to fit in here...

4. Look Who's Squawking!

Oh, and no matter what else you do—and even if you don't read a single one of the seven or so reviews coming up—please know that it's my solemn duty to inform you that you are not, I repeat, you are not allowed to scroll all the way to the bottom of this post. I mean, do not whizz right to the scoop on the dilemma facing your blogger, complete with a parrot picture like the one above, if that reminds you even remotely of the Monty Python Flying Circus skit where an irate customer goes to a pet shop to register his complaint about a dead parrot!)

Hint: The dilemma your blogger faces has to do with how —once the visitor count at our old-and-no-longer-maintained digs had soared past **100,000**—folks *still* keep going to our old blog site (aka our old digs) and not coming *here* (to our new digs.) What gives? Still scratching my head...

Anyhow, remember that you'll want to check out the reviews below first, as you merrily wend your way to the grand finale involving the scoop (flagged by the reappearance of the parrot picture above). And you're, like, *What?!*

5. *Forbidden Knowledge*

Listen, for crying out loud, I told you just a moment ago that you're forbidden from whizzing—aka blissfully and mindlessly scrolling at warp speed—to the bottom of this post. Surely you have the self-control to stay the course. No? Surely you have the will-power to delay gratification and (momentarily) keep away from checking out the happenings which involve an irate customer goes to a pet shop to register his complaint about a dead parrot. No?

Good luck with delaying gratification (that serpent in the garden), though something tells me that you *can* muster resolve: So while you grapple with *your* will-power dilemma, this one of your own making—and ready or not—we now dive into our reviews of the finest (book-format) wisdom that will help you navigate the rollicky Go landscape without sweat...

All buckled-up?

6. Book #1. The Go Programming Language by Alan A. A. Donovan and Brian W. Kernighan (Addison-Wesley Professional Computing Series)

This fine—though admittedly terse—book should be near the top of your list on the way to Go enlightenment. It is to Go what The C Programming Language was to C (No kidding, C is the grand-daddy of Go.) Having said that, I rush to caution you (especially if you're coming brand new to Go) against attaching anything more than (some) semantic similarity between the two languages (i.e. Go and C), because each of these two languages solves completely different sets of problems.

Yes, you may have heard that Go is the C of the 21st century; and yes, Go inherits from C its expression syntax (every bit as terse as that of C), its control-flow (whittled-down statements), its basic data types (compact and efficient), call-by-value parameter passing (never mind you, legions of Java programmers), pointers (should I even broach this subject before someone cries uncle!), and finally—as rightly pointed out by Donovan and Kernighan, the co-authors of this fine book—Go inherits (from the C tradition) programs which, "*compile to efficient machine code and cooperate naturally with the abstractions of current operating systems.*" (Lots more details, should you wish for more, that is.)

In full candor—and sterling though it is—reading *The Go Programming Language* has, at times, felt like taking medicine... Right there you should have a clue that this book is going to be good for you! (At least that's what I was always told: Medicine, especially the bitter one, is good for you!) Seriously, though, who reads programming language manuals for fun; trust me, if that's your idea of fun, more power to you. But at the end of the day, this (reference) book is indispensable, so you might as well warm up to it. Yep, resistance will be mostly futile. Not only that, this book deserves to be read several times, not once;

think of taking multiple doses of medicine. Makes sense? Surely you took all your medicines when you had to, right? What?! (OK, we're not going there…)

Segueing a bit: At my first job out of grad school—with Schlumberger—back in the day (1995), I did virtually all my programming in C. And just as *The C Programming Language* remained chained to my desk, nowadays *The Go Programming Language* plays that captive role instead. Doggone it, there's even some elegant beauty in its terse narrative, come to think of it, like the kind of austere beauty which a smart cookie (the British mathematician and philosopher Bertrand Russell) kept talking about, for example when he opined that

> *Mathematics, rightly viewed, possesses not only truth, but supreme beauty—a beauty cold and austere, like that of sculpture, without appeal to any part of our weaker nature, without the gorgeous trappings of painting or music, yet sublimely pure, and capable of a stern perfection such as only the greatest art can show.*

And to that I'll add another quality which this book shares, and not with medicine—I wanted to rule that out since we were chatting just a minute ago about how stuff that's good for you sure can taste like medicine—but with math: Rigor. A *lot* of rigor. Yep, this book is a keeper. (Just remember not to sleepily put your copy of *The Go Programming Language* in the medicine closet late at night. OK, so it's the *medicine* that goes in there; *books* go in your bookshelves, or on your desk, provided there's any flat surface available!)

7. Book #2. Learning Functional Programming in Go by Lex Sheehan (Packt Publishing)

This is the book that finally helped me get Go. What more can I say?

I was tempted to move this book to the top spot (on this list) but finally decided against that act as being too heretical; I mean, the canonical book—Donovan and Kernighan's *The Go Programming Language*—just *has* to have that honor (if for no other reason than that the legendary Brian Kernighan is one of its authors!)

Seriously though, and coming back to the book which comes in at the second spot—*Learning Functional Programming in Go*—let me just say this: I am simply stunned by the uniformness of its top-notch quality content. This isn't the kind of stuff that some really smart (Go) software practitioner just woke up one morning and wrote up; it comes from someone with deep industry experience, with tremendous insight into what makes programming tick, plus a mastery of explaining knotty concepts simply and with a pleasingly engaging writing style. Take this from someone (hey, that's yours truly, for crying out loud) who knows a thing or two about Functional Programming (aka *FP*, since using the minimum possible to stand in for the maximum possible is a core tenet of FP, going meta and a tad recursive here, heh)—and regular readers of this blog are likely fully aware of that anyway. So there.

OK, over here now, and back to our review: So this amazing book could not have come to my attention at a better time: I had dived deep into using the Go programming language last year (circa early-to-mid 2018), ramping up to work on an awesome open source (polyglot language) project hosted by The Linux Foundation: EdgeX Foundry (As a committer on EdgeX, I have been using Go exclusively, full time, for a while now; coming as I did from a deep background in Java and Scala (each an awesome language in its own way), I had to repurpose my programming style (and mindset) from the ground up to learn how to do things the Go way.

A word to the wise while we're at it: Go is *incredibly* opinionated, but in a genuinely good way. You will be relieved of drudgery and verboseness, plus end up feeling far more confident in truly understanding, among other things, what Rob Pike had in mind when he said—and I'm paraphrasing from memory here—that "*Less is exponentially more.*") It will take some time. Take heart, though; it *can* be done.

If you think about it—in the end—everything can be (and *should* be) related, simple, and well-designed. The biggest problem, IMHO, especially with FP, is that the smart guys who originally saw how it works, seem to have the hardest time making it easy to understand. But that's not a problem (in the least, whatsoever) with *Learning Functional Programming in Go*: Somehow it manages to capture tough ideas (think "essential complexity") and strips away their "accidental" complexity. And that's a *big* deal, if you ask me.

With a nod to the mind-bending observation that "*A language that doesn't affect the way you think about programming, is not worth knowing*" (by Alan Perlis, the very first recipient of the Turing Award), I am especially pleased to have this book by Lex Sheehan at my side as a trusty resource. Among other things, working intensively with Go has forced me to rethink what it means to leverage a programming paradigm in the service of creating great software that's designed to unfold, to emerge—so to say—and to delight customers.

You are bound to get a ton out of *Learning Functional Programming in Go*. I did. Don't miss it!

8. Book #3. Go in Action by William Kennedy, Brian Ketelsen, Erik St. Martin (Manning Publications)

In a way, this is a language lawyer's book: It dives remorselessly —without so much as wincing—into the guts of the Go language. To take just one example, in educating the reader about the innards of "slices," the authors let us in on the fact that "Slices are tiny objects that abstract and manipulate an underlying array." What makes it all hang together (as in this tiny example on the subject of "slices," and elsewhere throughout the book) are the copious and thoughtfully lavish illustrations.

Yes, there's a ton of helpful details (on the ins and outs of programming with Go) to be found between the two covers of *Go in Action*—which is why I bought it in the first place!—the narrative never gets bogged down, though. The authors somehow manage to keep things fun throughout by using copious examples that are well-chosen, thoughtful illustration, nicely annotated code, and stuff like that. It's not a big book; decidedly slim and compact. Methinks that you will want to check this one out.

9. Book #4. Programming in Go: Creating Applications for the 21st Century by Mark Summerfield (Addison-Wesley Professional)

This is an excellent, but often-overlooked book. Why it remains overlooked, I don't know: Maybe because its subtitle—Creating Applications for the 21st Century—puts programmers off as being too, um, "marketing"-speak or something? Seriously, though, Programming in Go: Creating Applications for the 21st Century is extremely well-written, so I would urge you to pretend that its subtitle doesn't even exist. (Gosh, this is getting a tad existentialist, and did I even bring this up? "Akram, how could you?!", I hear you say. Oops.)

Anyhow, one thing I like a lot about this book is the sure-footedness with which it fearlessly tackles the task of showing you how to internalize the mindset of programming in Go the way this language was intended and designed for. While I haven't read any *other* books by its author (Mark Summerfield), he is clearly a master expositor, paring explanations down to their essential complexity, stripping away extraneous—darn, I thought I had been doing good lately on the pact with myself to steer clear of **sesquipedality***—and accidental complexity.

What you get is a down-to-earth set of coherent narratives that have clearly been thoughtfully woven together in the service of educating the next generation of Go programmers. Calling all Gophers!

Whoa! A lightbulb just went off—what with my waxing lyrical about this book's vision of educating the next generation of Go programmers—and it dawned on me that similar thoughts must have surely made a foray or two into the collective consciousness of the marketing folks who came up with its dazzling subtitle—*Creating Applications for the 21st Century*. Hey now, I was just sayin'.

If I ever meet the author, I'm going to tell them what a splendid job he has done. Meanwhile, if you run into him first, could you please tell him that I said hello?

Hey, what are you waiting for? Go get this book. Now.

*Sesquipedality (is the use of big words, literally those that are "a foot and a half" long, according to Bryan A. Garner, in his fine tome called *Garner's Modern American Usage,* published by the venerable Oxford University Press.)

10. Book #5. Concurrency in Go: Tools and Techniques for Developers by Katherine Cox-Buday (O'Reilly Media)

A great second—or possibly even third—book on Go programming for you could be Concurrency in Go: Tools and Techniques for Developers by Katherine Cox-Buday. This delightfully written book makes, in turn, reading it a pleasure. Everything you ever wanted to know about Go concurrency is in here—all presented in easily digestible chunks.

Let's face it: Doing concurrent programming in *any* programming is hard, though Go makes that effort (considerably) more tractable with its amazing programming construct called "channels" (For more details, I invite you to check out: Some Of The Coolness Go Has To Offer) It's all inspired—*and* informed—by the notion of communicating sequential processes (CSP), which originated in Tony Hoare's wonderful white paper in 1978 (In a nutshell, all processes communicate and synchronize via channels.) What makes Go especially cool is that it's very core is permeated by CSP (again, think "channels".)

I guess all that is is a roundabout way of saying that we programmers still—and will conceivably *forever*—need all the resources we can get our paws on when it comes to concurrency. But rejoice. All the good stuff (and *no* fluff) are in this fine book by Katherine Cox-Buday. She is a gifted writer who knows well how to guide the reader through the thicket of concepts that are part of the (Go) concurrent programming landscape. To take one small example, here is just one of the (many) pointers that Katherine shares in the Preface to her book:

> *When I read technical books, I usually hop around to the areas that pique my interest. Or, if I'm trying to ramp up on a new technology for work, I frantically skim for the bits that are immediately relevant to my work.*

Now *that's* my kind of writing style, one that I'd be happy to sign my name to!

There simply isn't—and likely *never* will be—any pixie dust (who knows for sure, so we're calling Tinker Bell to be safe) that one wishes one could sprinkle on their codebase and make it magically concurrent. At least *I'm* not holding my breath for that kind of transformative agency! But the closest thing I've seen (in terms of clear, engaging, and thoughtful guidance in the area of Go concurrency) is right there between the pages of this fine book.

Enough said.

11. Book #6. Go in Practice: Includes 70 Techniques by Matt Butcher, and Matt Farina (Manning Publications)

Maybe Fleetwood Mac (hey, does anyone even recognize the name of the remarkable light-rock music group from the 80s?) knew a thing or two about Go programming back when they released their song Go Your Own Way, way before Go was a twinkle in the eyes of its co-creators (Rob Pike, and Ken Thompson, and Robert Griesemer.)

But I (nearly) digressed (And I'm hearing you loud-and-clear when you say, "Akram, stop, don't you even *think* of pulling off another one of your random digressions the way you wantonly did around on our old digs!") Heh, heh, *hey*, relax: There is a subtle—I was going to say *subliminal*, but bit my lips—*method* to this madness (i.e. my seeming digression to Fleetwood Mac). "Like, what?," you ask.

Glad you asked: So there is the *Go* way of doing things, and then there's *your* of doing things (Spoiler alert: *Never the twain shall meet.*) If you are coming to Go from a different programming paradigm (such as the object-oriented, imperative, or even the functional paradigm), much as I did about a year ago, then you're gonna find out quickly that there's a delta between the *Go* way of doing things and your way of doing things. Period.

And that's precisely where *Go in Practice: Includes 70 Techniques* comes in. The authors have done a pretty good job —with a reasonable amount of handholding—of showing what the Go way of doing things really *looks* like. While it's not all roses (i.e. the Go way of doing things), there definitely *is* a method to their madness in having designed Go the way they did (referring again to the three amigos: Rob Pike, and Ken Thompson, and Robert Griesemer.)

So take it from yours truly, somebody who's been there and done that: Save yourself a *lot* of needless pain in your practice of Go programming and get familiar with the 70 techniques explained engagingly in this book.

But if you *still* want to go your own way... Look, I'll be the last one to stand in your way. Just saying.

12. Book #7. Go Web Programming by Sau Sheong Chang (Manning Publications)

What, web programming with Go: Are you serious?! OK, so even if you never end up writing even a single line of web-centric Go code, don't pass up on this fine book: It's got plenty to offer to those who are not web developers. In fact—and this is likely what gets lost on most people when they glance at the somewhat poorly-named title (Go Web Programming)—this fine book has much to offer to back-end developers (which is the Go programming community, predominantly, I'd say.)

The author, in fact, pointedly notes in his Preface to the book that "*It's all about HTTP again and how to deliver content and data through it.*" So there you have it. Now go forth and tackle your eventual consistency concerns head-on!

Yep, the author gets the simplicity and refreshing directness of the language.

Superbly explained coverage of a bunch of topics (at just the right level of detail), topics that remain relevant to me on a daily basis—such as handling requests, processing requests, storing data, web services, and leveraging Go concurrency— make *Go Web Programming* a refreshingly welcome book. And yes, it's eminently readable—not at the same level as *Concurrency in Go: Tools and Techniques for Developers*, but not terribly far behind either.

If you want to understand the relevance of HTTP to your programming (at the gut level), *Go Web Programming* is the book for you. Let's all collectively forgive the somewhat ineptly-named title, and not pass up on its value proposition. This one's another keeper.

13. Book #8. C: A Reference Manual (4th Edition) by Samuel P. Harbison, and Guy L. Steele (Prentice Hall Ptr)

Wait a second: So what, exactly, is a book on C doing here (on a purported list of Go books)? My reasoning is twofold:

Checking if anyone is even awake-enough to notice the appearance of a C book (in a list of, yes, *Go* books)

Reminding you—and here I'm being told that subtlety is my middle name—that it's no coincidence that Go has been dubbed as the C of the 21st century.

And did anyone notice the name of the esteemed Guy Steele on the cover of this book? For those not familiar with his name, he just happens to be one of my all-time programming heroes— yep, right up there with (the late) John Vlissides—and is widely regarded as the father of Common Lisp. (Steele also happens to be the lead author of The Java Language Specification; by the way, he co-created the Scheme programming language while he was an undergrad.)

Should anyone be into writing operating systems code, by all means read this book; plus, learning C never hurt anyone (Ages ago, I *did* put up with a bunch of sleepless nights as I grappled with... C pointers!) At a minimum, check out *C: A Reference Manual (4th Edition)* to get a sense for what a magisterial writing style might look like when applied to technical subjects—think *Artificial Intelligence: A Modern Approach* (Pearson) by Stuart Russell (UC Berkeley) and Peter Norvig (Google).

14. Wait A Second...

"And surely you're joking, Akram? You snuck in a parrot while we weren't looking!"—Um, may I nudge you in the direction of scrolling down (past the parrot below) to find out?

15. Look Who's Squawking (Again!)

Finally, a word on our old blog site (aka our old digs)...

It is no more; I mean, the old blog site is still *out* there, but it *sure* isn't get updated (at least not by *me!*) So one more time—repeat after me—the old blog site is no more. Put another way, the old blog site has ceased to be! It has expired. Bereft of life, it rests in peace, etc. OK, let me spell this out...

Wait, and better still, allow me to point you to *Monty Python's Flying Circus*, in particular the episode where a customer (named "**C**", but of course) enters a pet shop, and has the following chat with the pet shop owner (named "**O**", but of course).

Read at your own risk, as it might be side-splitting funny, even as it manages to shed (some, and only marginal) light on how it came to be that your blogger keeps wondering why—once the visitor count at our old-and-no-longer-maintained digs had soared past **100,000**, thank you!!—folks *still* keep going to our old blog site (aka our old digs) and not coming *here* (to our new digs.)

Like, what's up with *that?* (Well, there's nothing like taking the tram below to a smidgen of the fabled skit from the one and only *Monty Python's Flying Circus*; I'll meet you on the other side as you disembark your tram ride.)

Aha, you made it to the other—dark—side! So let's dive right into a tiny snippet from that *Monty Python's Flying Circus* skit. (I'll wait for you while you do…)

So there you have it: My old blog site's metabolic processes are now history! That's actually an unerringly apt description since the content (on the old site) isn't growing, although it isn't shrinking either; for some reason, though, innocent folks keep flocking to *that* (old) site, and not *this* (new) one.

Waaah!! What am I doing wrong? Somebody? *Anybody?!*

16. Marveling At The
Designs Of Nature

To calm our (collectively) frayed nerves, we're going to do one thing, right now: We are going to treat ourselves to the soothing balm of nature, busily working away, hand-crafting ineffable designs (Our Go programs—or programs written in any other language, for that matter—can only aspire to be but crude approximations of the ineffable designs of nature. So go ahead, take in the blissful, organic growth in the pic below (It's a surreal-looking marvel that is a fine specimen of the Campanella species, which is a genus of fungi in the Marasmiaceae family—bottom-line is that you can stare at the mystic unfolding of nature; just make sure you don't eat any of that Campanella!)

So this post—hey, I still like to think of these critters that you all blithely call "posts" as "essays," really—was going to end now, except that...

17. Campanella

"Except what?" you ask, understandably so. Well, it goes like this: Methought I heard something 'bout Campanella! And I can't let that just go. You know?

So, you ladies and gentlemen out there in ether space, dear Readers that you all are—for crying out loud—the gloriously-named Campanile happens to be the (more) popular name of the famed tower whose *official* name is Sather Tower (a monumental and marvelous bell tower you'll find planted smack in the middle of the Berkeley campus of the University of California.) Read on if you don't believe me...

18. The Campanile

"Yeah right, Campanella, Shampanella, we don't believe a word of what you say, Akram!"

Hah, I knew, I just *knew* this was coming (my way, as in, *right* into my parlor). And I'm prepared. Woohoo! For picture proof that <u>I *was* there</u>, (at the *Campanile*, mind you, and not at the site of the *Campanella* genus of fungi, because I sure don't go near no fungal critters growing in any old underbrush) I invite you—yep, you all, fine ladies and gentlemen of the jury—to check out *Exhibit A* (the pic below).

19. Exhibit A

That's me in front of, yep, the Campanile. And should you perchance have not had enough of all this—oh my, the ravenously incandescent curiosity you all bring lights me up!—and want still more on my visit to The University of California at Berkeley campus (from a while ago), then allow me to point you to the following coordinates: Software Actors, Rare Benefactors. (Compelled by the mores of keeping the truth in advertising, I hasten to add: That essay is not all—or even mostly—about my visit (to UC Berkeley), but it sure has a bit of it.)

So once you have, in turn, visited the coordinates above, to check out the intriguing (and even beguiling) mysteries of software actors—that is, *should* your burning curiosity have emboldened you to undertake the danger-fraught, perilous pilgrimage—and you then decide to come back to *this* essay...

OK, *then* we need to talk some about the recursive aspects of experience as we know it (in the spirit of something like those bouncy Clojure trampolines). Just sayin' (But you *can* take me up on the offer, just not right now!)

◆ ◆ ◆

POSTCARD V: CREATIVITY: ALL YOUR QUESTIONS ANSWERED

0. Intro

I dwell in possibility.
~ Emily Dickinson (the best poet ever)

D ear Far-flung Friend,

I will have to ask you to seat yourself while you read this postcard. Ahem. So this *fifth* one—in the series of eight postcards from a fabled island built totally from software—we are about to enter the zone of meditation central, ala creativity. (That's what *I've* been doing anyway, woe betide, ever since I got stranded, smack in the middle of this alluring archipelago, the one with no zip code, no nothing...)
Truth sure is stranger than fiction. But we're going to be brave. Undeterred, we're about to take on the most vexing questions ever posed about a decidedly perplexing subject: Creativity.

Are You Sure?

It's right here, really: *Everything* you ever wanted to know about creativity. Yes, all your questions answered. (We don't leave out even a single one.) And all that, too, served up in the scant moments it would take you to feast on a bowl of cherries.
Isn't life sweet?
Alas, reality intrudes. I'm sorry to inform you that the bold statements made above were by someone else. Definitely not me. You see, *moi*, I don't do that kind of stuff. Why in the world

would I make the audacious claim that I've got answers to all the deep questions anyone has ever posed about the essence of creativity?

Yo, Creativity Czars

For one things, the creativity czars of the world would be out to scalp me. And I can't just let that investment (in my scalp) go down the tube, especially after years of putting up with the chore of tending to it with gobs of that foul-smelling *Head & Shoulders* shampoo. What to do now?

1. Disguises Up, This Very Second

Quick, lest anyone catch the drift—imagine Tarzan taking a super-deep breath through his flared-up nostrils in hopes of catching a spoor of predators—we are going to stave off the specter of scalping by artfully divulging all that follows under a pseudonym (By the way, and while stranger things have happened, I invite you to stay tuned for some pseudo-randomness in this very area—pseudonyms, that is—if you care about asserting the rights of writers, authorship, and that sort of thing.)

Let's pick an innocent enough name, and yet sounds like a world-renowned expert in all things creativity. How about Humbert Humbert? (That's right, the first and last names are identical: We want to really, *really* throw all those snivelers off our track lest they get a whiff of identity or authorship.)

2. Let The Questions Roll In...

Meanwhile, why don't we rack our memory to make sure we got that right—*Speak, Memory*, or forever hold your peace. Yeah, I do think we got all our ducks in a row.

Your quacks, I mean, *questions*—on all things creative—come in and Mr. Humbert dutifully answers them, one by one.

Here we go.

A man should look for what is, and not for what he thinks should be.
- Albert Einstein

3. On The Road To Creativity

Dear Mr. Humbert: Is the road to creativity a long and winding one?

Dear Sue-Irl Ng: Yes. Swirling, and that too sinuously, is exactly what the road to a more-creative you will be. Its serpentine track will lead you far and wide. On top of that, the road is amorphous; it will be decidedly fluid, in the sense that the road will mold itself to the unique tracks of the seeker who follows his or her own trail to creativity.

But not to worry. And lest all this is starting to sound *too* New Age—we sure don't do non sequiturs around here either—allow me to elaborate.

The fuller story, as it unfolds, has us scanning the horizon in search of landmarks—nope, not those roadside signs that tell you how far away your next outlet mall or rest area is. We're talking about being in this for the *long* haul; hence the need for signposts and landmarks.

But before you jump into that *U-Haul*, a word to the wise: Think of your journey to a more-creative you as the unfurling of a rose bud into a marvel of beauty and splendor, or the unfolding of a grubby chrysalis into an untethered and oh-so-graceful butterfly.

So yes, dear Sue-Irl Ng, we're grooving right into the tracks of that (possibly apocryphal) joke about a pedestrian in New York City asking the first musician he sees for directions, "*How do you get to Carnegie Hall?*", and gets the weary reply from the musician, "*Practice. Practice. Practice.*"

One more time, this time altogether, the answer to "*How do you become more creative?*" is, "*Practice. Practice. Practice.*"

Yes!

With that, I urge you to stay the course, a long and winding one that it surely is (Do hold on to that Carnegie Hall metaphor with all your might.) Moving on to the other questions we see trickling in...

Oh, I nearly forgot to mention, but if you come to a fork in the road, take it.

Invention is the talent of youth, as judgment is of age.
-Jonathan Swift

4. On Its Renewability

Dear Mr. Humbird: Is creativity a renewable resource?

Dear Enner Gee: Funny that you should ask. I happened to be gazing at a picture of some lovely wind turbines scarcely a minute ago (elegant at least to an *engineer's* mind.) What's baked into that pic, but left unstated, is a glimpse into processes that warrant constant replenishment. For example, sunlight or wind keep shining and blowing, respectively, their availability depends on time and weather, of course. Automaticity writ large in the service of constant replenishment, amirite?

(What's this? Aha, I see a slip being handed to me, alerting me to how the ill-advised use of mannerisms—these confessionals, amirite?—can inadvertently divulge a person's identity. Sigh, we may just have busted our pseudonymous subterfuge.)

But we are not cowered. Onward.

(By the way, it's Mr. *Humbert*, not Mr. Humbird—I neither hum nor am I bird, and definitely not a hummingbird at that, if those hovering critters are what you had on your mind.)

Yep, much like you—and here I assume that you, too, are presently under the impression that creativity is somehow inherently renewable—yours truly, too, had labored for *years* under the same illusion! So allow me to burst the bubble: There's nothing automatic whatsoever about the renewability of creativity. Nope. Nothing of that sort.

So yeah, there's nothing inherent in creativity which would lend itself to making it automatically renewable.

But there *are* a set of four pillars—I recently heard them being brilliantly formulated as such by a trusted friend—which you can erect and thereby enable the edifice of creativity to stand robustly, and for creativity to *thereafter* become renewable: As *The Boss* has been known to say, you can't start a fire without a spark.

So yes, first we crawl, then walk, and finally run. (*That's* how we do it.)

And not to be dogmatic, but those traits—think of them as the pre-conditions which must be met to have a balanced equation "unfurl" itself out into a renewable whole—are the very pillars upon which creativity can be advantageously founded. In no particular order, those traits, then, are:

- Curiosity (*Or, a fire to be lit*)

- Passion (*Or, sticking your neck out*)

- Devotion (*Or, what are the ways that I may serve thee?*)

- Humility (*Or, let me sit at your feet to learn*)

More light will be shone on this delicate and elusive matter, I'm sure, in the course of our taking on more questions, so keep the faith. Meanwhile, allow this paradigm to sink in (pillars and all!) and be comforted in the knowledge that laboring under that illusion we talked about at the outset—that creativity is inherently renewable—is decidedly *not* a raw deal.

We may skin our knees into rawness every now and then, dear Enner Gee, but we also *grow* as we learn. Paradigm shifts happen.

The journey *is* the destination, after all. And while there is no royal road to creativity, there *is* a way. It's not easy, but we're up for it, right?

We're warming up now. Let's bring on more questions.

I have no special talent. I am only passionately curious.
~ Albert Einstein

5. What About Curiosity?

Dear Mr. Humburg: Would you please tell us something about curiosity—the first of the four pillars upon which you had opined that creativity is to be founded—and how to cultivate it?

Dear Q. Rheus: Goodness, we have here a fellow lover of my beloved em-dash—I regale in your masterful use of those lovely grammatical critters in posing your question—so let me be the first one to welcome you to the show. And just so you know, don't *you* go anywhere.

(By the way, it's Mr. *Humbert*, not Mr. Humburg. I don't look like a hamburger, do I?)

There's an abundance of material, actually, on this very topic. Head straight for the following handful of coordinates to check out

- *The Tao of Creativity*

- *Lit Gets Tech Makeover*

- *Tech Gets Lit-Smitten*

Once you've checked that stuff out, dear Q. Rheus—go ahead, I'll wait for you right here—you will probably realize that, yes, we've written *quite* a bit on that topic; maybe a bit *too* much. Our readers are totally satiated: Adding more material on top of that would be sheer folly. And we're not going there.

But yeah, the *TL;DR* on this is that cultivating curiosity is akin to kindling a fire. It's a fire to be lit.

6. And What Of Cultivating It?

Dear Mr. Hummer: Will you tell us of the ways of cultivating passion in the service of a more-creative me?

Dear Dylan Thomas: Certainly. I will share what little I know about this most elusive of the four traits that form the bedrock of creativity—passion—notwithstanding the long-standing tradition of everyone (and their brother!) taking the liberty to opine ad nauseam on what this passion thing is all about.

(Sigh, one more time folks, it's Mr. *Humbert,* but I suppose you can call me that... Oh dear, what in the world is generating all this kinda eventually-consistent pseudo-randomness when it comes to pseudonyms; not that *I'm* using one, amirite? Darn, gotta be careful about slips of the tongue in the area of those oh-so-endearing mannerisms.)

Anyhow, dear Dylan Thomas, you keep on rage, rage, raging against the dying of the light—I'm sure you've got good reasons for not going gentle into that good night. Me, when bedtime rolls around, I don't think twice: I repair to get my beauty sleep.

Oh, by the way, when allergies season arrives in Wales, and should you get those bedtime sniffles, I suggest that you go with herbal remedies. Just don't take *Nyquil,* unless you really, *really* have to. Not being owlish here; thought I'd share the tip because *Nyquil* sure could put a damper on your nocturnal raging.

Seriously, though, passion—the kind that will keep you motivated to soldier-on in the face of adversity—comes from a place of deep desire in the human heart. It's almost the opposite of fads; the fad will not be for you, lad. So if you're the kind who follows the latest fashion, than you might as well forget about passion.

Put another way, dogged perseverance comes from deeply-felt desire. It comes from a sense of conviction. You feel it in your bones.

And it all begins with finding something you truly believe in, something that brings you joy. And when you find that special something, you have to believe in your own self. You'll know that you've found it—that special something—when the prospect of putting in those proverbial 10,000 hours fades into the distance as a minor detail. With you fired-up, boredom goes out the window, because

> *Boredom is just the reverse side of fascination: both depend on being outside rather than inside a situation, and one leads to the other.*
> *-Arthur Schopenhauer*

Above all, remember that cultivating passion is *not* at all about competing with others; it's *all* about competing with your own self, to see how far you can push yourself in search of excellence in your chosen field.

Put another way, dear Dylan Thomas, you take it to the limit. Then you do it again. And again—later, rinse, and repeat.

The *TL;DR* here would be that cultivating passion (in the service of a more-creative you) is having the guts to stick your neck out and the gumption to have a skin in the game.

Of the night for the morrow,
The devotion to something afar
From the sphere of our sorrow.
~ PB Shelley (in his poem One Word Is Too Often Pro-
faned)

7. 'Tis The Magic Fuel?

Dear Mr. Humdinger: When it comes to fostering creativity in oneself, is it true that devotion plays a role in "fueling" the magic?

Dear Deevo Shen: You got that one right. Yes, devotion is about imbuing a sense of service. Devotion is all about bringing nurturance into the equation, and doing so with the poignant tenderness with which mama bird and papa bird tend to their fledglings they've helped procreate.

It's warm, it's fuzzy. Most of all, it's real; you can bet your bottom dollar on that!

Devotion just may be the polar opposite of the scams that unscrupulous individuals will try to sell you on, with promises of making a quick buck. Making a buck—in fact, making *lots* of bucks—is perfectly fine. It's just that money is a poor motivator for cultivating the kind of devotion we're talking about.

Take it from yours truly, Mr. Humbert—sigh, it's a humdinger, but I've grown used to having people call me by all sorts of names—that the subject of money is one that I strongly advise you to *not* bring up with the proprietor of this blog (in the context of advertising and that sort of thing which lies on the slippery slope at the periphery of true content.) Over the years, I have come to believe this guy Akram truly thinks that devotion is the next best thing since sliced bread.

But I digress. (Hey, that's not my lingo: That proprietor dude made me say that! Me, I am, of course, Mr. Humdinger, I mean, Mr. *Humbert*, and *I* surely never digress. So there.)

Look, let's leave the question of identity to the realm of the lovely, literary mysteries populated by the likes of famed detective Sherlock Holmes and his faithful friend Dr. Watson. Closer at hand, as we cruise around the ins and outs of cultivating devotion in order to become more creative, I recommend that you to get yourself a copy of a stellar—and often-overlooked—book by Joyce Carol Oates entitled *The Faith of a Writer*. It may well be some of the best money you ever spend.

In particular, I invite you to check out a section (in *The Faith of a Writer*) where Oates introduces a marvelous, brief, and altogether tantalizing passage from John Updike's autobiographical book *Self-Consciousness*.

There's something magical about devotion. Then again, there is no royal road to creativity; you have to beat your own path and carve out a passage through the thicket. Your unique acts of devotion—ones that only *you* can identify, and I know you're up to it—will make the arduous task of carving a passage through the thicket that much easier.

Devotion, dear Deevo Shen, then, would, for its TL;DR, be imbued with the sentiment inhering in the rhetorical question, *"What are the ways that I may serve thee?"* (And would you like some fries to go along with that? Darn, the dining meme—I must be getting hungry.)

Tell you what, though: Let's take a few more questions while we're on a roll. Food can wait for a bit.

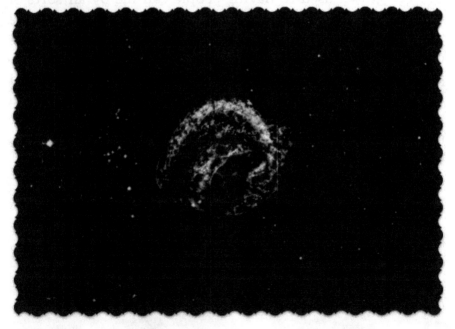

The fittest may also be the gentlest, because survival often requires mutual help and cooperation.
~ Theodosius Dobzhansky

8. This Thing Called Humility?

Dear Mr. Hummerson: Will you now tell us something of humility—the *fourth* of the four pillars upon which you had opined that creativity is to be founded—and how to cultivate humility in the service of fostering creativity?

Dear Hannibal Humble: You—and me along with you—now stumble on to a crucial yet often-overlooked trait, one that has much to offer in the quest to become more creative.

Let's go a tad meta here. You will be like the tree that gives shade to the passersby who take rest under its canopy. Wait, we're not done yet: The part having to do with hitching your wagon to a star comes later. (Hold your horses, partner.)

You see, I could easily have chosen the realm of software architecture—my, excuse me, *Akram's* area of expertise—but let's broaden our horizons and take an example from the realm of writing. Look, nobody is born a Dickens or an Oates or a Faulkner. We all have to start somewhere. Somewhere humble. First we read, then we write, right? (Akram's telling me right now to replace that trailing "right? by the more fashionable "amirite?", and get me in trouble. But I ain't doing that. Hah. No sir. Not *me*.)

So yeah, we all start at the pastry cart. (Goodness, my stomach continues to growl. And I want to roll and rumble, dear Hannibal Humble. But I'll stick around just to answer your question!)

What I really meant to say was that we all—at least the writers among us—start cultivating humility through the sincerest form of flattery: imitation. I'm not making this up; would-be writers up and down your street are at this very moment trying to imitate *their* favorite writers as they hone their own craft. The good ones succeed. But the great ones, in their quest to imitate, end up failing.

But guess what? *Even* as they fail at imitating their favorite writers, they end of doing something wonderful and strange:

They wind up creating a truly original piece of work that's strikingly original, strange perhaps, but beautiful in conception and originality, wondrous in its strangeness.

They came looking to imitate their heroes—and heroines, to be sure—out of sheer admiration; they ended up creating art.

You, too, can do it.

(Meanwhile, I'm telling you, that guy *Akram* is looking over my shoulders to make sure it's really *me* writing this stuff—Sheesh, he's a stickler for authentic expression, though I could never really tell what he was reading on any given evening.)

Moral of the story: Stay humble, dear Hannibal Humble. Work with devotion. Put in the hours. There's no such thing as an overnight sensation.

So the *TL;DR* here would be that cultivating humility is the sentiment that would accompany the pronouncement, "*Let me sit at your feet to learn.*"

(Have *I* ever digressed? Oh no, not me. But as an aside, that Dobzhansky quote atop this dialog—"*The fittest may also be the gentlest, because survival often requires mutual help and cooperation*"— is something I encountered while scouring the field of Polyvagal Theory. As an avowed bagel-lover, I even proposed the rubrics of a *Polybagel* Theory which, alas, did not quite leaven as much I had wished for it to; an ill-starred Baker's dozen, perhaps.)

Our chief want in life is somebody who shall make us do what we can.
~ Ralph Waldo Emerson

9. A Different Drummer?

Dear Mr. Humdrum: Do creative people march to the beat of a different drummer?

Dear Dee Dum: Fiddlesticks. Nothing of that sort, dear Dee Dum. Next question?

You cannot put a fire out;
A thing that can ignite
Can go, itself, without a fan
Upon the slowest night.
~ Emily Dickinson

Dear Mr. Humberson: Can we perhaps imagine creativity as a vessel, which, when filled with the "fuel" of the four traits you have enlightened us with—curiosity, passion, devotion, and humility—could be used to refactor a problem (or a challenge, or even a vision) into something new and more-tractable?

Dear Wize Won: You've asked a deep question. For crying out loud, you're making me rethink my *entire* conceptualization of this creativity business. I thank you! (By the way, do you usually have Trix cereal for breakfast? *Just* asking.)

Why, this is beautiful. The way you formulated your question is making it all come together; the pieces of the puzzle are fitting together. A full picture is emerging. This is heady stuff. Stand back.

We take five deep breaths. We take it all in.

Eureka!

This is what we need to do to "conquer" creativity: We fill-up our fuel tank and never stop filling—imagine if you will a vast storehouse of experiences which has infinite capacity and can always take on *yet* more experiences, a bit like the fabled Hilbert Hotel which always that can always take on additional guests, even *infinitely* many of them.

Do that kind of fueling (*and* refueling) long enough and the engines of your ingenuity are bound to roar even if you end up shy of notching infinity (Sorry, Hilbert Hotel custodians about all those tips you'll admittedly miss out on.) But yeah. You guessed it: Your creativity *soars*.

So get those oars out, dear Wize Won, and start rowing like crazy. (With an oar in each hand, we will set sail on the nighttime sea, and maybe even write an ode or two during times of respite, under the glow, of course, of those magically luminous fire-flies.)

TL;DR says: "*Fill 'er up.*"

But let there be spaces in your togetherness.
~ Kahlil Gibran (in The Prophet)

10. Something Of Fostering?

Dear Mr. Humvee: Does Kahlil Gibran's utterance about letting there be "spaces in your togetherness" have any bearing on fostering creativity?

Dear Starry-eyed Sarah: So the other day I spotted a bumper sticker on a Harley-Davidson motorcycle pungently proclaiming that *"If I Have to Explain, You Wouldn't Understand"*. Not being trained in the science—art?—of metaphysics, I feel inclined to curl up like a porcupine and let my quills announce my reluctance to engage in matters such as the one you bring up here.

Wait, there's this guy though...

Yes! I remember now: His name is Akram—fiddlesticks, it rhymes with "drum"—and oh boy, can *he* tell tales! Go talk to him about such matters (at your own risk, I hasten to add) and he'll help you connect dots where there were (seemingly) no connections to be made. Even if the oceans dry up and the earth shrivels into an iota—imagine a world replete with vertices, yet wholly devoid of connecting edges—that guy will help you make connections.

Remember what I said, though. Once you get him started... (Just sayin.)

Speaking of the deuce, just the other day he was excitedly telling me about hearing some profound thoughts that touch upon the theme here: Gesturing animatedly with his arms in explication—or maybe he was simply fighting off an airborne infestation of horse-flies above his head—he could scarcely hide his excitement in sharing some talk he had heard from a friend (yep, the excited chap we're still talking about is the same deuce whose name rhymes with the drummer boy's drum. Dee dum, Akram.)

Anyhow, the gist of that talk was that we need to ponder more; there are some areas of cognitive dissonance in describing creativity as an artifact of pre-conditions. Explicitly downplaying the inhibitors of creativity, specifically: (1) ego, (2) hanging on to existing paradigms as doctrine, (3) not taking a step back to view a given problem through the macro-micro lens, (4) overwork or stress, and (5) overly uni-dimensional focus on a specific area.

Wow. I'm smitten by the clear-eyed thinking. What more can I add to that glory, dear Starry-eyed Sarah, except to remind you, in the words of the Sage of Concord, to *"Hitch your wagon to a star."*

Think of the fierce energy concentrated in an acorn! You bury it in the ground, and it explodes into an oak! Bury a sheep, and nothing happens but decay.
~ George Bernard Shaw

11. What Do Creative
People Eat? Really.

Dear Mr. Hamilton: Is it true that creative people have *Trix* cereal for breakfast?

Dear Beatrix Potter: ARGHH! Somebody get me out of here: One more question reminding me of food—there goes my stomach, growling again as a potent reminder of just how famished I must be—and I press the "Eject" button. (I'm sure they have one of *those* around here, even though they don't offer complimentary snacks to guests like yours truly, Mr. Humbert—or, I guess, Mr. Hamilton, to you.)

Sigh.

Since you ask, creative people *do* have a marked propensity for working energetically; they're only *warming* up while others are closing shop. Either they—the creatives, you know—have monumental supplies of good old *Trix* cereal stashed away in their desk drawers or they're not good at keeping track of time so don't know when to stop. (Or maybe both!)

At any rate—and you can witness that important-looking official in the pic above ratifying *"Trix-for-one-and-all!"* into law— the future is bright for *Trix*-munchers. They may (or may not) march to the beat of a different drummer, but they sure got their priorities right when it comes to selecting wholesome, nutritious elements from the food pyramid.

Should you, dear Beatrix Potter, say fiddlesticks to that, let me remind you that the *Energizer Bunny*, too, has been known to regularly (and slyly) wolf down *Trix* morsels. And you know how *that* bunny—the perpetual-motion machine that it is— keeps going and going and...

Hmm... Beatrix Potter... Your name sure sounds familiar...

Wait, is it *you* who wrote a ton of books involving furry bunnies hopping all over the countryside or something?

Methinks I don't stand a chance against an onslaught from

hordes of feral rabbits. Help—Somebody sign me up for that witness relocation program I heard you all talking about!

Out beyond ideas of wrongdoing and rightdoing there is a field. I'll meet you there.
~ Jelaluddin Rumi (Sufi poet extraordinaire)

12. Where Do They Hang Out?

Dear Mr. Humswung: They say that a rolling stone gathers no moss. But really, where *do* creative people tend to congregate?

Dear Field Stone: I don't know. And frankly, at this point, I don't care. You don't give me any food. No snacks for the guest. No nothing. On top of that, my host subliminally bombards me with questions laden with themes suggestive of mouth-watering goodies.

It's too much for one person to take.

My stomach, for crying out loud, dear Field Stone, continues to growl, growling into a widening gyre; the centrifugal force is a bit much for me to continue defying...

I choose to press the "Eject" button.

"WHOOSH!"

To conceal anything from those to whom I am attached, is not in my nature. I can never close my lips where I have opened my heart.
- Charles Dickens

13. What! Gone Fishing?

Dear Mr. Humsing: Can creativity be likened to the tendrils of the jellyfish inasmuch as the leitmotif holds water when it comes to going deeper (and deeper still) into the substrate where creativity can gain purchase, scaffold-like, and thereby blossom and burgeon?

Dear Langwidge Lover: We regret to inform you that our guest —the illustrious Mr. Humbert—has left our premises in a huff, without exchanging so much as a word. He did slap on top of that blue table over there a rumpled slip of paper on which he evidently scribbled something on his way out the door. Let's see, the slip says...

"Gone fishing."

Oh my. Sorry, dear Langwidge Lover, but the subtext there seems to be that you're up the creek, without a paddle. Please hang up now, and try your call again later.

Character develops itself in the stream of life.
-Johann Wolfgang von Goethe

14. We Debrief

We Emerge Unscathed

Now *that* was quite a pickle we just got ourselves out of, wouldn't you agree? That business of writing under a pseudonym, something told me, was snake-bitten from the start, beset at its outset as it was by the equally flustering business of pseudo-randomness: Our poor pseudonymous guest (Mr. Humbert Humbert) sure got the deal of his life as he tried to field the penetrating barrage of questions with which he was bombarded, even as he was called by names—Humsing, Humvee, Humberson, and Hummerson were only a few of those names—that were any but his *own*.

To make up for that (asinine asymmetry in the unfolding of events unannounced), we are going to honor his presence—all of the 30 minutes that he graced our digs—by a replica of the picture that had marked the onset of our trek. Yes, scroll down some to behold one more time that selfsame, long, and winding autobahn.

A Choice To Be Made

And as it appears into view, let yours truly—I've been called a sprezzatura by my well-wishers and also some *less*-charitable names by the *not*-so-much-well-wishers—leave you with the words of the French philosopher Jean-Paul Sartre when he remarked that

One must choose whether to live one's life or tell it.

The choice is yours. You have to live a life that's right for you, not merely an aura (of you and your life) that somehow *sounds* right. Do you want to *tell* your life rather than live it?

You see, the world is packed with people just like you and me who have made—and continue to make—choices solely because they thought it would make their telling of their life that much "cooler."

Can we resist such temptations? Can we shut our ears to the siren calls of fads and fashions? There's got to be more to life than that.

Enter creativity.

Creativity And The Authentic Self

Imbued with the wherewithal of the oh-so-elusive stuff that is creativity, I am firmly of the opinion that we *can* repulse those siren calls which can—and *will*, if heeded in folly—buffet us in the treacherous seas of distraction. So let's you and I choose to resolutely swim with the currents of our authentic self. Shall we?

Let's refuse to be anyone but ourselves.

Embracing creativity can—and *will*—help us in this area.

The seas can be choppy and the road long and winding—depending on how you view the journey metaphor—but there's no better time than now to begin your own journey to a more-creative you, a more-fulfilled-you.

I won't even pretend that I have the answers—let alone *all* of them—but let's you and I rig our worlds for creativity, always reminding ourselves that

> *Character develops itself in the stream of life.*
> *-Johann Wolfgang von Goethe*

◆ ◆ ◆

POSTCARD VI: TECH GETS LIT-SMITTEN

*Smite, smote, **smitten**;*
We got magic mittens.
~ Akram Ahmad (a decidedly *lesser*-known poet)

*He had **mittens**, Minjekahwun,*
Magic mittens made of deer-skin;
When upon his hands he wore them,
*He could **smite** the rocks asunder,*
He could grind them into powder.
~ Henry Wadsworth Longfellow (a positively
more-well-known poet)

0. Introduction

Dear Far-flung Friend,

It is my fervent hope that you emerged unscathed after our communal immersion in the realm of meditation central last time. Feeling all creative now, right?

I say we celebrate by taking a lighthearted stroll down an avenue lined with mystery and intrigue, enveloped in the commingling of tech and literature.

What A Combo

Wow, talk about a combination. But don't take my word for it. Go ahead and take a dip for yourself. Me, that's all I do, having gotten stranded on a fabled island from where I keep sending you postcards...

Write back, won't you? It's rather lonely here. Meanwhile, let's check what happens when—as I alluded to a minute ago—we draw close to the commingling of tech and literature.

Ah yes, this was bound to happen... What with lit getting itself a tech makeover—and an extreme one at that—the last time around, there was no way that tech was going to be left behind. Oh no! Nobody outdoes programmers. Nobody.

So yes, in some sense, all this was inevitable.

Oh, The Unbearable Lightness Of It All

So here we are, about to embark on the journey of a lifetime —prepping ourselves to soak in the wisdom of a generation—

as we begin to lower ourselves into the gently lapping waves of the ocean whose innocent surface belies leagues of mystery and intrigue shrouding the hitherto unrevealed details of how tech got lit's *mitten*. Wait. I surely meant to say, "how tech got *lit-smitten*." Yeah, that sounds better.

We're all ready, I say, for our deep-sea descent. Oh yes, we are ready for a splash!

1. The Incandescent Descent

At this time, I urge you to take a few deep breaths and ingest only in small pieces everything that follows, lest you get the bends. Here we go, lowering ourselves into the sea of mystery and intrigue which have, to this day, enveloped the commingling of tech with lit.

We start divulging the juicy details (starting with Shakespeare doing eventual consistency) at 20,000 leagues under the sea, and don't stop until we reach the depths—descending all the way to the near-unfathomable depths of the Mariana Trenches —and get the scoop on a Silicon Valley tale as told to me by the Brothers Grimm themselves:

- Piece #1: Shakespeare Does Eventual Consistency

- Piece #2: Sherlock Holmes On Debugging

- Piece #3: JK Rowling Casts DevOps Spells

- Piece #4: Charles Dickens Is Beguiled By Clock Synch

- Piece #5: Thoreau Does Refactoring, Thoroughly

- Piece #6: The Brothers Grimm Tell A Silicon Valley Tale

You tracking me so far?

2. Piece #1: Shakespeare Does Eventual Consistency

To be eventually consistent, or not, that is the question:
Whether 'tis nobler to suffer transactional inconsistencies,
Or to let go the comfortable numbness of transactional guarantees
The slings and arrows of outrageously expensive warranties,
Or to take arms against a sea of ACID troubles
And by opposing end them. To converge—eventually,
No more sloppy quorums; and by a hinted handoff to say we end
The heart-ache and the natural shocks of lossy write availability;
That flesh is heir to replicas: 'tis a consummation of shards
Devoutly to be wish'd. Count monotonic reads—and sheep—to sleep;
To sleep, perchance to dream—ay, there's the rub:
For in that monotonic sleep, what dreams may come, of sharding
When we have shuffled off this mortal, multi-leader replication,
Must give us pause for garbage collection—there's the respect
That makes calamity of so long life;
Stop the world, O grim reaper in garbage collector's garb,
For who would bear the whips and scorns of replication lag,
The oppressor's wrong, the proud man's cross-datacenter link,
The pangs of handling write conflicts, the law's delay,
The insolence of the unmoored Schrödinger's Cat, and the spurns
That patient merit of a clawing, hot standby, loudly crashing,
When he himself might his inconsistent queries make
With a bare bodkin? Who would bear the requested API version,
To grunt and sweat under a weary two-phase commit,
But that the dread of something after a Byzantine fault,
The undiscovered, unacknowledged messages, from whose

bourn
No traveler returns, puzzling the system administrator,
And makes us bear the subsequently redelivered messages
Then fly to other data centers that we know not of?
Thus conscience does make cowards of us all,
And thus the native hue of last-write-wins conflict resolution
Is sicklied o'er with the pale cast of linearizable concerns,
And enterprises of great pitch, especially thine data-warehouse
vendors
With this regard their service integration attempts turn awry
And loose the RESTful aspects of action.
Verily, then, eventual consistency can be a good thing—
You see, nothing is good or bad, but the thinking makes it so.

3. Piece #2: Sherlock Holmes
On Debugging

We chance upon two of our friends—the famed detective and his sidekick—sitting on either side of the fireside at the sleuth's Baker Street lodgings, evidently engaged in deep conversation:

— **Sherlock:** My dear Watson, the time has arrived to tell you all about the finer points of debugging computer programs.

— **Watson:** Wussup, Holmes?

— **Sherlock:** Yo, should you wish to debug—and unsnarl—the snarliest of your programming bugs, mark my words, and follow the advice I'm about to share.

— **Watson:** Bro, but first tell me it ain't so?

— **Sherlock:** What?!

— **Watson:** Like, shouldn't we, first of all, divulge to the gentle reader that *this* is how we actually spoke back in London town, amirite? That is, before Sir Arthur Conan Doyle tiptoed in and started dressing up our language in fancy clothes...

— **Sherlock:** Sigh, let's take it one day at a time; today, we do debugging, and *only* that.

— **Watson:** Bro, I'm with you on this one. *And*, of course, with everything else that you say; I'm your sidekick, after all.

— **Sherlock:** Listen up, Watson, for these are grave matters, whose untoward neglect has led many a man astray.

— **Watson:** Gosh, I'm all ears. Plus this should teach me a lesson to come around to your your Baker Street lodgings perhaps *less* often, though I find myself irresistibly drawn to doing exactly that!

— **Sherlock:** My dear fellow, a certain discretion would befit you more.

— **Watson:** Don't you pay any attention to what I just said. Do carry on.

— **Sherlock:** So here's the deal: Once you eliminate the impossible, whatever remains, no matter how improbable—

such as buffer overflows, SQL injections, improper validation of an array index, and even those pesky null pointer dereferences —must be the truth.

— **Watson:** You don't say, bro?

— **Sherlock:** I do. And there's more.

— **Watson:** Gulp. Tell me, boss.

— **Sherlock:** My dear fellow, life is infinitely stranger than anything which the mind of man could invent.

— **Watson:** Well, the Chicago Cubs are predicted to win the World Series, you know...

— **Sherlock:** Hush, boy. Get your mind out of the rut of sports. I'm about to impart forbidden knowledge; it is for *your* ears only. Come closer and listen carefully.

— **Watson:** Okay, boss. But but next time please use that mouthwash.

— **Sherlock:** Listen up. We tread on dangerous ground, with software development costs overrunning corporate budgets out the wazoo, breaking the backs of corporations—all because of a disheartening lack of training in the art of debugging computer programs.

— **Watson:** You mean it's no longer halal and kosher to ship software products once the software project compiles?

— **Sherlock:** No, my boy, no.

— **Watson:** Great. *Now* you tell me, with my team and I having just emerged from pulling all-nighters these past two weeks and shipping a major upgrade to London's stock trading software!

— **Sherlock:** Buddy, you work your own method, and I shall work mine.

— **Watson:** Pray continue, dear Holmes; that was a minor detail, anyway.

— **Sherlock:** You will, at all times, remain cognizant of the dictum that debugging is more—dude, way more!—than "*making the bug go away*".

— Watson: Darn. *Now* he tells me...

— **Sherlock:** Hush, boy, don't be so impudent. You must groove with the empirical approach: using the software itself to alert you to what's going on. Plus, hang on tight to the rigor of the debugging process (reproduce, diagnose, fix, reflect).

— **Watson:** Sounds halal and kosher to me.

— **Sherlock:** We don't have much time on our hands, so let's get cracking on the steps of the debugging process, starting with reproducing...

— **Watson:** Whoah, Holmes, you surprise me at times; am I, like, about to get a good old refresher on the birds and the bees?

— **Sherlock:** No, my dear fellow, I speak not of procreation; it is in the sense of reproducing *bugs* that I seek to enlighten you.

— **Watson:** I'm tracking you now, boss. Pray continue.

— **Sherlock:** Elementary, my dear Watson. Just as most everything nowadays is on-demand—on-demand movies, on-demand water heaters, on-demand interviews to name just a handful—what you've got to do is apply the same idea to debugging and find a way to reliably and conveniently reproduce the problem (on-demand!)

— **Watson:** Um, does this tie in to the supply-and-demand curve perchance?

— **Sherlock:** Hush, Watson, you digress (Leave that sort of thing to the author of this essay).

— **Watson:** Say, boss, can we pick up the rest of the debugging process—diagnose, fix, reflect, and stuff like that—some other time?

— **Sherlock:** Sigh, I surmise that you just might be a ten o'clock scholar, Watson.

— **Watson:** Say what?

— **Sherlock:** Watson, must you be so ignorant in matters of nursery rhymes?

— **Watson:** Boss, the matter is urgent...

— **Sherlock:** Oh, why didn't you say so, then?

— **Watson:** Ah, perhaps I *should* have: My iPhone pizza-tracker app was telling me that our delivery of anchovies-laced, personal pan pizza is well on its way to 221-B Baker Street, yay!

— **Sherlock:** Woohoo! Forget all about debugging.

— **Watson:** Say what, bro? Oh, and I was getting ready to ask you

about the pizza crust—was it supposed to be pan, thin, or thick?
—plus impress you with my emerging ideas based on my tangential research into the thickness of the Procrustean Bed.

— **Sherlock:** On with the real stuff of life, the one around which we must gather: Let's make hay while the sun shines, dear fellow. And remember to tip the delivery boy because he's real chummy with my prim landlady, the one-and-only Mrs. Hudson; otherwise, she will be on my case. Again.

With that, our two friends—the famed detective and his sidekick—head straight in the direction of the best that life has to offer: pizza slices dripping with cholesterol.

4. Piece #3: JK Rowling
Casts DevOps Spells

Today, I'm here to tell you the story of the versatile spells—all in the fine tradition of JK Rowling's's Harry Potter series—spells whose incantation can summon help when we need it most, which is more often than not especially when dealing with Dev Ops glitches.

Here, then (and by popular demand, in the *"Problem-Solution"* format of *"Glitch—Magic Spell"*) is a fine selection of such versatile spells as will make your head spin when you see the ease with which we accomplish our mission and extricate ourselves out of vexing scenarios.

Glitch: A database with fine-grained permission models to control access (e.g. PostgreSQL) is being recalcitrant and locking up unpredictably. How to unlock it?

Magic Spell: Yell Alohomora loudly and it will immediately unlock and open all the doors you ever wanted to (or not.)

Glitch: The wily intruder has dropped a payload on the target servers. The payload is some kind of backdoor script or malware small enough to be downloaded and executed without attracting attention. The backdoor applies the instructions and attempts to move laterally inside the network, scanning and breaking into other hosts until it finds a valuable target. How to make it move downward whereby the intruder can be exposed and contained?

Magic Spell: Calmly utter the word Descendo, which will cause the target object to move downward.

Glitch: Most applications need to receive some kind of secret as part of their configuration. How would such a service receive the cryptographic keys needed to encrypt the data, and do so in a way that quickly limits services with secrets whose size exceeds the maximum length of environment variables?

Magic Spell: Wryly repeat the word Engorgio, which will engage the Engorgement Charm, causing objects to increase in size.

Glitch: Cloud providers often provide a mechanism by which a transferred key provides no more security than if we had passed decrypted configuration files directly. They (i.e. cloud providers) also provides a solution to this problem through its Key Management Service (KMS), a cryptographic service. But how to efficiently apply this to (seed) objects chosen at random?

Magic Spell: Simply utter the word Portus, and witness any old object transform into Port keys!

Glitch: What kind of a method, statistical or otherwise, can help reduce the noise in the data, and only trigger alerts when clients violate predefined thresholds?

Magic Spell: No problem, just say Silencio to make interfering noise go silent.

Glitch: Information-disclosure threats are a royal pain because they involve exposing information to individuals who aren't supposed to have access to it—for example, the ability of users to read a file that they weren't granted access to, or the ability of an intruder to read data in transit between two computers. How to make the guilty party levitate and thereby divulge their identity?

Magic Spell: Love this spell rolling off of my tongue each time I utter Wingardium Leviosa and engage the Hover Charm, which causes an object—any object, oh yeah!—to levitate

Hey, what about *Muffliato*, the spell used to prevent conversations from being overheard by filling the ears of those nearby with an unidentifiable buzzing noise?

5. Piece #4: Charles Dickens Is Beguiled By Clock Synch

It was the best of times, it was the worst of times; it was the best of times because the US Women's Soccer Team, the trail-blazing American patriots led by Megan Rapinoe, had chalked up another awesome victory by winning the Women's World Cup 2019, and it was the worst of times because a bug had been discovered in NTP (the Network Time Protocol), whose clock synchronization between computer systems over packet-switched, variable-latency data networks was found to unravel ever few milliseconds.

It was the age of wisdom, it was the age of foolishness; the age of wisdom because the industry as a whole remained firmly committed to developing software according to SOLID principles, and the age of foolishness because people everywhere foolhardily kept looking for free lunches despite being up-braided for paying scant attention to Moore's law having maxed out!

It was the epoch of belief, it was the epoch of incredulity; deep belief networks in general and deep learning in particular had powered us smack into the frenzy of a genuine revolution, but fake news was scorching and gaslighting the soul of society, not to mention the fruits of the aforesaid revolution serving such lofty pursuits as turning to social media in general and fake-books in particular to find out whose pet's coiffure had garnered the most likes that day.

It was the season of Light, it was the season of Darkness; light-weight, agile development approaches had gained traction, but our society remained benighted by the ever-stretching shadow cast by the moving target that is code bloat.

It was the spring of hope, it was the winter of despair; func-tional programming, along with the arrival of the remarkable Go programming language, had sprung on us from unbeknownst quarters, but feature creep, alas, was not going away anywhere, anytime soon.

We had everything before us, we had nothing before us; quantum computing was on the horizon, but our entire stash of Domino's Pizzas coupons had expired.

We were all going direct to Heaven, we were all going direct the other way; domain-driven development was gently leading us away from the yellow brick road, but the telltale footprints of DLL hell, sigh, had not tiptoed away, yet.

In short, the period was so far like the present period, that some of its noisiest authorities insisted on its being received, for good or for evil, in the superlative degree of comparison only; ah yes, notwithstanding how Twitter had, to its everlasting credit, contributed the amazing Apache Storm stream processing software framework to open source, the social media platform that it powers had, alas, been hijacked by some of the noisiest rabble-rousers imaginable.

6. Piece #5: Thoreau Does Refactoring, Thoroughly

While the strategies associated with refactoring—that's the process of changing a software system in such a way that it does not alter the external behavior of the code yet improves its internal structure—were conceived in Smalltalk circles, it wasn't long before they found their way into other programming language camps. In particular, another camp which refactoring strategies made their way into was the one which Henry David Thoreau had set up on the shores of Walden Pond (It was actually a wood cabin, but that's merely a minor detail, amirite?)

Anyhow, I'm here today to tell you the unknown story of how Thoreau immersed himself in a bunch of refactoring tactics—and yes, I meant to say *tactics*, not *Tic* Tacs. Here, then, by popular demand, in *"Problem-Solution"* format, is a segment of that story (Hey, I can't give all of it away now!)

Problem #1: [The Code Smell here is: Primitive Obsession] You see, and so said another sage by the name of Martin Fowler, "people new to objects usually are reluctant to use small objects for small tasks..."

Solution #1: Consider the wise words of the Sage of Concord (more like a problem restatement, if you ask me, but...) when he said, "White Pond and Walden are great crystals on the surface of the earth, Lakes of Light. If they were permanently congealed, and small enough to be clutched, they would, perchance, be carried off by slaves, like precious stones, to adorn the heads of emperors; but being liquid, and ample, and secured to us and our successors forever, we disregard them, and run after the diamond of Kohinoor. They are too pure to have a market value; they contain no muck. How much more beautiful than our lives, how much more transparent than our characters, are they!"

Problem #2: [The Code Smell here is: **Bad Smells in Code**] Kent Beck and Martin Fowler "If it stinks, change it." Grandma Beck—

relation of legendary programmer Kent Beck—discussing child-rearing philosophy.

Solution #2: Aha, this one is simple if you only hearken to the words of Thoreau when he said, "What is the pill which will keep us well, serene, contented? Not my or thy great-grand-father's, but our great-grandmother Nature's universal, vege-table, botanic medicines, by which she has kept herself young always, outlived so many old Parrs in her day, and fed her health with their decaying fatness. For my panacea, instead of one of those quack vials of a mixture dipped from Acheron and the Dead Sea, which come out of those long shallow black-schooner looking wagons which we sometimes see made to carry bottles, let me have a draught of undiluted morning air. Morning air!" So there you go, in two words: "Morning air!"

Problem #3: [The Code Smell here is: Lazy Class] Again, in the words of the eminently fine gentleman Martin Fowler, "A class that isn't doing enough to pay for itself should be eliminated."

Solution #3: A bit more abstract than what we've seen so far, but not rocket science either if you follow Thoreau when he opined that, "The greatest gains and values are farthest from being ap-preciated. We easily come to doubt if they exist. We soon for-get them. They are the highest reality. Perhaps the facts most astounding and most real are never communicated by man to man. The true harvest of my daily life is somewhat as intan-gible and indescribable as the tints of morning or evening. It is a little star-dust caught, a segment of the rainbow which I have clutched."

Problem #4: [The Code Smell here is: **Inappropriate Intimacy**] "Sometimes classes become far too intimate..."

Solution #4: A (seemingly) tough nut to crack, but only so if you forget what the Sage of Concord reminded us pithily when he said, "One inconvenience I sometimes experienced in so small a house, the difficulty of getting to a sufficient distance from my guest when we began to utter the big thoughts in big words. You want room for your thoughts to get into sailing trim and run a course or two before they make their port. The bullet of your thought must have overcome its lateral and ricochet motion and fallen into its last and steady course before it reaches the ear of the hearer, else it may plow out again through the side of his head. Also, our sentences wanted room to unfold and form their columns in the interval."

7. Piece #6: The Brothers Grimm
Tell A Silicon Valley Tale

Once upon a time, many, many moons ago, a critical mass of physicists—you know, the kind of scientists who wear white overcoats and scurry around corporate laboratories and clean rooms as if they're engaged in stuff of paramount importance? —had a bunch of time on their hands and decided to invent the electronic transistor.

And thus was born the modern digital world. Remember the magic beans that Jack planted in his backyard? And how that bean stalks grew and grew and grew? Yep, so did the transistor emerge from the laboratories and start making its way into applications that nobody could have imagined. And its applications branched out. In fact, their reach was incredibly diverse, and their applicability just grew and grew and grew as if there was no tomorrow.

Fast-forward a bunch of decades—and I mean a *ton* of decades —and we got ourselves computer programs outstripping their fledgling status and become super-sophisticated beasts in their own right. These trends continued right up till this very day when we find deep learning having taken the industry by storm; the allied technology is so advanced that it fulfills each one of Arthur C Clarke's Three Laws, especially the third one (*"Any sufficiently advanced technology is indistinguishable from magic"*).

Oh yes, a bunch of industry sectors nowadays depend on deep learning algorithms—all traceable to the back propagation algorithm, the stuff of my MS thesis from many moons ago— which map inputs to outputs by forming nonlinear mappings of immense complexity, complexity which computer scientists at the forefront of the field are furiously tackling so as to reverse engineer their inner workings.

Oh my, how our beanstalk grew!

But wait, isn't there supposed to be a big, bad giant in the story, the one that Jack had to escape to save in his life? Yes, George Orwell foretold a big part of that in his dystopian novel named 1984. Big Brother is watching us; maybe it's that giant of bean-stalk infamy himself. He ain't no brother of mine, though!

Tell you what, everybody lived happily ever after—we're talking fairy tales, for crying out loud. Except there's a warning, which is this: We've got to make sure that we don't get done in by deep fake technology; and you thought we had it bad enough with fake news swirling around!

The End

◆ ◆ ◆

POSTCARD VII: TO ITERATE IS HUMAN

0. Intro

Work consists of whatever a body is obliged to do. Play consists of whatever a body is not obliged to do.
- Mark Twain

D ear Far-flung Friend,

In this, my penultimate postcard—you *do* read them, don't you?
—you get an up-close-and-personal look into what happens
when one soul (yours truly here) remains exposed to the elements of nature, one day too many.

At any rate, hey, I count my blessings, and say: Let's get started
with an altogether fleeting digression (and those are the best
kind, dare I say), a digression to the hilarious *Parkinson's Law*.
Clearly, I'm getting increasingly creative in finding ways to keep
myself—and, in the process, *you*—entertained.

I Pine Away

And hey, you *still* haven't written back to me? What's up with
that? (Oh, maybe a problem with those pesky zip codes, eh?)

No worries, and while we're busily ferreting away some of that
lovely work—come to think of it, there's even a naughty for-
mulation by the name of Parkinson's Law which would have us
believe that work expands so as to fill the time available for its
completion—I say it's time to take a break from scaling walls of
text (over here on our blog, that is).

I Turned To Look But It Was Gone...

Hear ye, all those present, especially those seeking refuge, if only momentarily, from the digressions we do here—mostly the doings of your truly—this is your moment. Revel in this fleeting freedom that is now yours!

Yep, we're going visual this weekend.

Heh, lest your jubilation be an overextended one—and before you run that jubilant victory lap to celebrate this respite from digressions—let it be known that the good stuff (digressions, what else?) can return unannounced any day now, at a moment's notice...

1. *This Is How It All Began*

Anyhow, it all started—this thing about erring, iterating and re-cursing—innocently enough, with an old chestnut to the effect that

To err is human; to forgive, divine

Hmm... Given the compact size of the saying above, more a wal-nut than a chestnut. But I digress (already!)

2. Forgiveness Morphed
Into... Recursion!

Curiously enough, that old chestnut about erring and forgiving —most likely having been waylaid by recursively zealous computer science aficionados such as the soulful-eyed, innocence-feigning one in the pic above—morphed into the likes of how

To iterate is human; to recurse, divine.

Oh my.

3. *It Was Off To The Races*

Along came your blogger—a self-styled essayist of sorts—and then we were cooking with gas. Speaking of cooking, and should you have the stomach for this sort of thing, I say, let's sally forth and witness the results (Ahem, all at your own risk, I hasten to add).

And in the process of reading (and digesting) what I've cooked up for you, should you cringe, please remember: We're merely on a visual binge.

So there.

Disclaimer: Every single variation (on that walnut-of-a-saying about erring, iterating and recursing) which follows are *my* doing—thereby adding to my sins of commission, taking a break from those of omission—and nobody else's. Yep, nobody does this sort of thing better, amirite?

To net time might feel inhuman; to waste it, you just go online

To woo and rue is altogether human; to moo, bovine

*To have our vision blur is but human; to C#, **Go Forth** unto sunshine*

*To **deburr** a roof aloof is human; to woof, canine*

*To demur is human; **to concur**, applaud the divine*

To splurge is human; to purr, feline

*To **read essays** is human; to **write them**, mighty-fine*

*To bedraggle in **WET software** is altogether human; to keep it **DRY**, oh-so-frontline*

*To **nab a saboteur** is human; jab one, and you get a whine*

*To curse is bad enough already; to **re-curse**, asinine*

To do bland cuisine is de rigeur; to haute cuisine, there's kelp and brine

Ah, to head for the mezzanine and get that no-frills seat number nine; but to do it with style and quills, best to have a porcupine

If the 80s were, well, the 80s; this must be (multicore) cloud nine

4. Our Rickshaw Drops Us Off

I mean, we've tortured language enough already; it cried uncle, for crying out loud. Plus the rickshaw driver won't have anything more to do with us anymore. You know, the driver of one of those turbine-powered turbo vehicles? As in growlingly ferocious turbine, beloved the world over by felines and even more so by canines of any stripe you care to define.

5. Concentric Circles Of Carp

What's up with the design, I say? It's mighty fine and all that. But, really? Salmons go up the incline, while I pine for streams that could be mine (and definitely not thine). And you? Oh well.

6. A Room With A View

Reserve one for me, will you please? Send me the bill, which I will neatly underline, refine, and—goodbye dollars—sign.

Oh, and just in case you've trudged to the very end—it verily betokens the end of our tether—I must spring forward and congratulate you; you are far braver than I.

◆ ◆ ◆

POSTCARD VIII: BEST SCALA BOOKS (2019)

0. Intro

*Nature is an infinite sphere of which the center is every-
where and the circumference nowhere.*
- Blaise Pascal

D ear Far-flung Friend,

Our commune now draws to a close, and I couldn't bring myself
to part with you before imparting at least *some* value to you,
what with your having plunked down good money, right?
So in the hope that what follows will be edifying—hope springs
eternal in the human breast, especially if you find yourself
stranded on an island, I'm telling you.

About That *Search* Party

Take it away. And if you don't hear back from me, please send a
search party, won't you? I will be eternally grateful; after all, I'm
not building a stairway to heaven.
Speaking of which, behold the prospects of *finding* some
stairs; like, everywhere! That's because the word "Scala" comes
from the Italian word for stairway. So we're going to keep our
eyes peeled, lest we stumlble on one.
Seriously, though, here's the deal: Polyglot programming is in.
Totally in. In an epic way.
The (mostly) artificial divisions foisted upon the siloed ecosystem of programming languages are melting away; the hoary,

mossy walls—check the pic below for proof, should you care—
are coming crashing down. Watch out, Humpty Dumpty.

1. Where Have We Been?

Let's see where we've been, as an uber programming community, so we can gauge better where we are heading. Yo, on second thoughts, methinks that such an undertaking is going to engender a whole new essay; let's leave that for another time, shall we?

Today—and before I introduce the glittering gold that is the best set of (newer) books in the finest Scala geek entertainment —we will first glance at a *past* set of really cool (Scala) books with which we had some fun a few years ago.

The glorious past regaled us in gems such as these:

- *Programming Scala: Scalability = Functional Programming + Objects* (O'Reilly), by Dean Wampler and Alex Payne

- *Scala in Action* (Manning) by Nilanjan Raychaudhuri

- *Scala Cookbook: Recipes for Object-Oriented and -Functional Programming* (O'Reilly) by Alvin Alexander

- *Scala in Depth* (Manning) by Joshua Suereth

- *Functional Programming in Scala* (Manning), by Paul Chiusano and Rúnar Bjarnason

- *Scala for the Impatient* (Addison-Wesley), by Cay S. Horstmann

Okay, so those books *won't* reappear on this new list. Having said that, *each* one of the abovementioned books has aged well and is well worth your time.

And oh yes, the fun is back, red hot. Even that bike yonder is glistening in its new sheen, bedaubed crimson, in hues unforetold. Heady stuff: Woh!

2. *Ushering In The New Breed*

With that, let's roll out the cool, new stuff. These are a handful of books that I've devoured over the past five years or so. Having done a hilarious thing like that—brah, leave this sort of thing to your truly—I sense some vindication in reporting a simulacrum of what I saw at the (programming) revolution:

- *Programming in Scala: A comprehensive step-by-step guide,* Third Edition by Martin Odersky, Lex Spoon, and Bill Venners (Artima)

- *Scala Design Patterns: Learn how to write efficient, clean, and reusable code with Scala,* Second Edition by Ivan Nikolov (Packt)

- *Scala Puzzlers: The fun path to deeper understanding,* by Andrew Phillips and Nermin Šerifović (Artima)

- *Scala for Data Science: Leverage the power of Scala with different tools to build scalable, robust data science applications,* by Pascal Bugnion (Packt)

- *Scala for Machine Learning: Leverage Scala and Machine Learning to study and construct systems that can learn from data,* Second Edition, by Patrick R. Nicolas (Packt)

Oh, as for our running metaphor of stairs, let's throw in a nice, pagoda-like portal, shall we? With that, check the oh-so colorful pagoda below, framed in the background by... the Eiffel Tower! What's up with that?

3. *Abandon All Hope, Ye*
Who Enter Here

Just kidding (so don't you pay any attention to that macabre title above.) What I am saying, though, is that you will need to generate some motivation—hence the "hope" trope sans Bob Hope—and recalibrate your mindset to get up to snuff with this stuff. And I have full confidence in you, just as I had in myself when setting out to conquer this material.

Fear not, cuz here we go. Starting with an awesome boat-anchor-of-a-book, here's a bunch of books that I've devoured over the past five years or so...

4. Book #1: Programming in Scala (Third Edition)

When this book's authors claim—as they do in the subtitle—that it's comprehensive, they really, really mean it: I have yet to see anyone outdo this fine tome for its comprehensiveness when it comes to covering Scala in all its rich detail. Remember, applications abound.

"Hey, what's that fine, blue-emblazoned china teapot doing alongside my copy of the book as it stands tall on one of my stair steps?", you ask. Glad you did, because you're going to need a *whole* lot of brewed tea to make it through this epic volume on Scala—particularly so if you wish to do so in a state of mild wakefulness.

Turning again to the picture above, you will spy from taking a peek at the towering canopy of colorful, ragtag tape-flags that I've managed to affix—as in "plaster"—to the upper-right region of my copy of this tome, that this book is a keeper.

It's nothing less than a masterpiece of didactic brilliance (Channeling the late John Vlissides' awesome take on such matters.) Trust me, the pages are replete with readable gems; virtuosity on full display.

Programming in Scala (Third Edition) delivers the goods: If you grab only one book from this list, make it this one!

How about we check some cool (Scala-style) designs now?

5. Book #2: Scala Design Patterns
(Second Edition)

I read the first edition of this amazing book, cover-to-cover, when it first came out, and was blown away by the high quality of the content. I was especially impressed by the clarity of presentation.

Well, in the second edition of the book, all the goodness is still very much there, *plus* several improvements. Frankly, this is one of my all-time favorite (technical) books that has only gotten even *better*!

Scala Design Patterns is simply a pleasure to read. As its subtitle—*"Learn how to write efficient, clean, and reusable code with Scala"*—rightly claims, its pages are replete with copious amounts of nicely annotated code which nicely illustrate the ideas at hand.

The coverage of design ideas—cast in the Scala mindset—is remarkable both for its quality and quantity, and one in which Ivan has shared some of the highest quality Scala (production level) that I have seen to date. Superb coverage of design patterns (which you will find yourself quickly relating to) can be found in its pages.

I thought I knew a thing or two about Scala, but was pleasantly surprised to learn a *bunch* of great ideas to level up my coding skills and design repertoire!

Well done, Ivan Nikolov: We look forward to your next book!

Now on to an interlude filled with... puzzles!

6. Book #3: Scala Puzzlers

Here's a book that is bursting with fun. If you liked—as I sure did!—its Java cousin that goes by the name Java Puzzlers, you're going to like Scala Puzzlers a lot.

It's not perfect—for example, I would've liked to seen more on —but it stays true to the claim its title makes ("*The fun path to deeper understanding*".)

Each of the two coauthors is eminently qualified for crafting this tantalizing ragtag of fun (Scala) puzzles. Nermin Šerifović is an active Scala community member, and he organized the Boston Area Scala Enthusiasts user group; Andrew Phillips is a longstanding open-source developer and community member specializing in concurrency and high-performance applications.

What I'm getting at—with my preceding blurb—is that this book is a compendium of quality material. No fluff in here.

You don't *have* to read *Scala Puzzlers* to become a better programmer, though you'll inevitably find yourself moving in that direction, be prepared to find your mind stretched.

And now it's time to cast our eyes heavenward in order to catch a glimpse of the gleaming skyscrapers and spires erected by data science, powered by—you guessed it—Scala and its libraries.

7. Book #4: Scala for Data Science

Quite broad in scope, this fine book will help you gain awareness of some great Scala libraries out there. Both programmers and data scientists will find a bunch of useful stuff in its pages

I would advise you to keep in mind that *Scala for Data Science* is geared to help you grok programming with Scala's _functional programming capabilities_ placed front-and-center in its narrative, which is kind of cool—the way I look at it, if you're going to program in Scala, you *might* as well tap into its impressive parallel computing capabilities, not to mention how dozens of lines of code (in your favorite programming language) will likely melt into a mere handful of Scala lines!

I invite you to check out its superb coverage of the *Breeze* library in particular.

Oh, and while you're at it, be sure to also have a look at tapping into a functional wrapper called *Slick*, which, dare I say, will give you a unique insight into how one can work with stored data almost as if you were using Scala collections, all the while giving you complete control over when a database access happens and which data is transferred. Pretty cool, eh?

Disclaimer: If you spied that bright, saffron, squish ball in the picture above, please know that it, too—like its peers that appear in other pictures in this essay—is holding its own when it comes to symbolism. Indeed, is there to remind us of just how malleable ("squishy"!) practice of data science is, both in kind and degree, as we slice and dice through seemingly endless reams of data.

The coverage given to the Actor model of programming—specifically, getting a solid grip on concurrency using Akka—was interesting and instructive. Let's put all those multicores to good use, shall we?

Data scientists who have wondered what Scala brings to the table (as a tool for doing data science) can start with skimming through this book. They won't be disappointed.

Meanwhile, programmers of all stripes—yep, that's you and me —can rejoice in this good book through subtitle says it all: *"Leverage the power of Scala with different tools to build scalable, robust data science applications"*

Hang tight, our final stop is coming up next: Yo, let's keep climbing those stairs while we are at it!

8. Book #5: Scala for Machine Learning (Second Edition)

First things first: This intense book is not for the faint of heart. Having said that, I hasten to add that it's intense in a good way that will not overwhelm you.

This is a workhorse of a book that I though remains sure-footed in accomplishing the claim of its subtitle, which is a mouthful: *"Leverage Scala and Machine Learning to study and construct systems that can learn from data."*

Scala for Machine Learning will give you plenty of opportunity to go through some fairly intense functional coding, all in the service of machine learning and "stuff like that."

In full candor, the narrative of this book run somewhat unevenly, but don't let that deter you from checking it out: A good number of design ideas—the Scala way, of course—are to be garnered from its pages.

"But what's up with that Matryoshka doll?" I hear you ask, *"Yes, Akram, the gleaming red, brightly painted one, standing upright, right next to my copy of the book."* Glad you asked: That's a subtle reminder of the power of nested function calls (aka recursion.) Okay now—read my lips—no more spoilers, so go grab a copy and check what's happening for yourself!

And that's all we got for you this time. Hey, all good things come to an end, so perk up: Let's all look the part of our friend the stoic—*and* spunky—pelican who bids us farewell.

AKRAM AHMAD

TESTIMONIALS

I nearly left this section out—we geeks tend to shy away from talking about ourselves, don't we? So yeah, the only reason I did decide to retain this section is to level-set, because chances are that you haven't heard of me: Sort of to help you get to know me a bit better (and where my ideas and I come from. "*Go to the source,*" as this adage from programming circles would have it, amirite?)

With that, here are some blurbs—and here I headed over to my LinkedIn profile to grab a handful of testimonials—ones that you just *might* find interesting. (Should you start to tire, *please* feel free to sail right past this stuff, and jump into the book proper!)

One more time, we're just breaking the ice at this point...

Gerum Haile
Vice President -Chief Platform and Cloud Architect at USAA- Chief Technology Office
August 14, 2017, Gerum worked with Akram in different groups

I had the pleasure of working with Akram at Boston Scientific/Guidant and Ebay/PayPal. Akram is an excellent engineer that is technically sound, passionate, result oriented and team player. In addition, the drive he has on improving his craft through continuous learning sets him apart from most engineers that I have worked with in my career. Any technology organization(small , medium, large) can benefit from Akram's well rounded and superior technical and soft skills.

See less

Kamal Choubkha
Vice President, Product
Development- Workflow at
CCC Information Services
May 15, 2018, Kamal worked
with Akram in different groups

I have known Akram for over two years during which time we worked on implementing a new platform at CCC. I have been consistently impressed by Akram's attitude and productivity. Akram is both very bright and exceptionally motivated a person that any manager will love to have him as part of their team. Akram made major contributions to designing, developing, and operationalizing our hyper-scale platform, leading to a real-time application deployed to the cloud, which consumes and processes real-time streaming telematics data from IoT devices at scale, based on a technology stack which includes Apache Kafka, Storm, Zookeeper, DynamoDB (the NoSQL database), and REST web services in Java. He played a key role in successfully bringing in-house a significant codebase (from a startup acquisition), helped transition incoming developers into the corporation, and migrated the code-base (from an Eclipse-OSGi bundles-based build) to a standardized Maven build. The application continues to serve one of the largest insurance companies in the world. Also as part of the Architecture team, Akram performed POCs (Proof Of Concepts) on a routine basis to assess the viability (and feasibility) of incorporating emerging tools and technologies into the corporate stack. He created the base foundation of the (RESTful) Java application which performs vehicle damage-detection AI with customer-friendly "heat maps". Akram led the training of the extensive Chicago-based Development teams (as part of the Learning Academy seminars) to present and roll-out the Java application framework paradigm. Akram also has a highly popular blog ("Programming Digressions") that has a lot of useful information. I recommend Akram highly and without reservation.
See less

Beverly Mundy Weable
Senior Business Analyst /
Scrum Master
June 1, 2018, Akram worked
with Beverly Mundy in the
same group

I had the pleasure of working under the same leadership team as Akram in 2017 at CCC Information Services. While we never worked directly together on the same Scrum Team, his skills and enthusiasm were well-known across our group. It was our greatest desire to have Akram on our team. The management team had other plans. Once you see some of the stellar accomplishments from his tenure at CCC, you will understand the plans they had for him, for example: (1) Akram played a key role in migrating a massive code base from a startup acquisition to a standards-driven build in Maven (the popular build tool for the Java ecosystem). This particular software application serves one of the top three insurance companies in the country, (2) Akram is deeply invested in knowledge-sharing as well as, of course, enthusiastically acquiring that knowledge in the first place, which he then freely shares with others: He is a voracious reader, writer, and organizer of information and has applied these passions to his extensive project documentation which he made sure were easily accessible on project Wikis. He also authors a fun and fascinating blog where his broad interests in literature, culture, technology (and software design and development, of course) combine in essays that delight, intrigue, and teach his vast legions of blog followers. Treat yourself to some of his writings at his blog site, which is named "Programming Digressions", (3) Most importantly, Akram is an enthusiastic and positive force for all things good. The fact that he made such an impact on me—a Product Owner on a different team in a different office (based in Chicago, Illinois, and with him being based in Austin, Texas—says so much about his cross-functional collaboration and team spirit. Those are some of Akram's accomplishments that come to mind. There are many things I miss about CCC Information Services; but one thing I don't miss is Akram, and here's why: He remains a positive presence in my life, both as a friend and as a supporter of my career. He is a rare treasure! See less

Akram is a high caliber software engineer you can aways depend on during those critical high pressure technical challenges. He has deep knowledge of software design and application architecture which ensures your projects are rock solid right from the start.

We worked together on designing and building a number of high performance, high availability applications and platforms employing the latest research and technologies which supported millions of remote clients.
All these applications were build with sufficient layers of abstraction that worked in the cloud but could very well be ran on bare metal infrastructure which ensured portability and avoiding vendor lockdown.

As part of our group, which was specifically formed to acquire new markets, we constantly looked at the latest academic research and constantly created POCs to try new ideas. Akram worked on many of these new ideas and made breakthroughs which brought a considerable competitive advantage to our clients.

Akram is also a talented writer, I've always enjoyed his essays especially his book reviews on various software design, programming languages and technologies. He's read everything there is under the Sun on technology and culture which always made for very exciting and informative conversations.

In sum, Akram is a passionate software engineer with vast experience who enjoys his craft and always happy to share. See less

Okay, that'll do for now. (In all seriousness, though, I am *oh-so* humbled by these—and other—testimonials I've received over the years. I *truly* am, straight up from the heart!)
And hey, it was so nice to meet you (again), dear Reader.

AFTERWORD

Is this the promis'd end?
- Kent (in William Shakespeare's King Lear)

Though we have come to an end—and this just might be *"the promised end"* which King Lear had in mind with his utterance above—let's seize this moment as a *beginning* instead.... We'll treat this as merely *an* end, and not *the* end. The way I see it, the journey has only begun, amirite?

Along the journey, you may well have wondered, *"Man, all those pictures..."*. So yeah, there's a whole another story in there. (A story for another time, to be sure.)

What Did You Think?

Meanwhile, I thank you for sharing your precious time, for spending it lingering over these pages as you lavished your attention on the content. I can only *hope* that you got (substantial) value out of it...

Meanwhile, a little, island-bird—aha, it's the same one we met back when setting sail at the outset of this voyage—it tells me that the book you hold will be the one you lug with you if, heaven forbid, you get stranded on the proverbial desert island.

And please be sure to share your reactions (say, via a review on

Amazon) and to spread the word.

Surely you will want to read more—and I just might decide to write more—so why don't we keep this dialog going?

I Invite Contact

So yeah, do let me know what you would like to see in future books. (As a cue about possibilities, recall how it's been said about the programming language Lisp—the ultimate, *programmable* programming language—that *"Lisp isn't a language, it's a building material"*, in the words of the legendary PARC computer science researcher Alan Kay.

So there you have it, a *potential* theme for our next meeting over our *next* book. Dare I say that a combinatorial consideration of the commingling of languages—the natural kind (the ones we speak in) and the synthetic (the ones we use to program computers)—might offer us a glimpse into vista hitherto unseen? Juxtaposition to the rescue, amirite?

Hold on to that thought... And farewell, for now.

MY COORDINATES

B e in touch. My coordinates are as follows. And much as I remarked earlier, I invite contact—via any and all of these:

Blog → Programming Digressions: Essays
LinkedIn → This is a good way to stay in touch with me
Twitter → I occasionally do tweet
Email → It's there, *should* you wish...

AKRAM AHMAD

www.ingramcontent.com/pod-product-compliance
Lightning Source LLC
Chambersburg PA
CBHW071243050326
40690CB00011B/2238